Women's Higher and Continuing Education: An Annotated Bibliography with Selected References on Related Aspects of Women's Lives

Esther Manning Westervelt,
Executive Codirector of the National Coalition for Research on Women's Education and Development

Deborah A. Fixter,
National Coalition for Research on Women's Education and Development

with the assistance of Margaret Comstock

College Entrance Examination Board, New York, 1971

Copies of this book may be ordered from Publications Order Office,
College Entrance Examination Board, Box 592, Princeton, New Jersey 08540.
The price is $1.50.

Editorial inquiries concerning this book should be directed to
Editorial Office, College Entrance Examination Board, 888 Seventh Avenue,
New York, New York 10019.

Library of Congress Catalog Card Number: 74-174883

Printed in the United States of America

Contents

Introduction

To historians of some future time one of the most curious paradoxes of the twentieth century may be that rapid diversification of modes of communication paralleled a great upsurge in the flow of the printed word. This torrent has reached what seems today, in comparison with earlier centuries, flood proportions, yet there is every indication that the crest has not been reached. The myriad uses of radio, television, and data processing supplement but do not as yet replace books and articles as means of communicating ideas and knowledge.

Bibliographies have become invaluable aids to all but the most highly specialized scholars. Bibliographies of literature pertaining to women, while rather later in appearing than those in other fields of interest to scholars and practitioners, are becoming more common. Mounting interest in problems of women has generated a new spate of publications on the subject and has also augmented the need for bibliographic guides. Bibliographies obviate journeys to search for hours through long index drawers crammed with cards, or through numerous items listed under a multitude of headings in publications of abstracts. But to serve as short-cuts to sought-after material, bibliographies must have a limited scope.

"Women" make up a very large population. The variety of material pertaining to them is almost as infinite as women's own variety is reputed to be. Thus the most useful bibliographies focus on one or another area of women's lives and activities. The present compilation was prepared for scholars whose primary interest is in women's higher and continuing education.

To choose a focus for a bibliography does not, however, automatically take care of decisions about what is "relevant." There is a sense in which everything is relevant. Education, which is the focus here, is only one aspect of a woman's development; it not only affects her whole development but is affected by all earlier phases of it. The authors of this bibliography resolved this dilemma by deciding to place major but not exclusive emphasis on material directly pertaining to women's higher and continuing education and to place secondary emphasis on material pertaining to women's employment, which is closely interrelated both with aspirations for education and utilization of it. We place tertiary emphasis on materials pertaining to social and cultural roles, psychological development, and to those sex differences in characteristics and behavior that are clearly pertinent to education. Least emphasis has been placed on background material relating to women's status. References to other currently available bibliographies in specialized areas are included for readers whose concern for women's education may lead them into other areas of study pertaining to women.

The usefulness of bibliographies depends at least as much upon selection as upon collection. Items in this bibliography's area of primary focus—education—have been selected for quality, representativeness, and timeliness. Materials cited range from statements of opinion through descriptions of programs to research findings, but none are cited that seemed too ephemeral, superficial, or trivial to merit the attention of a thoughtful reader. Almost surely some worthwhile contributions to the literature have been accidentally overlooked, despite a painstaking search of all available sources of information. Some sound works have been omitted because they are of questionable relevance to women's higher and continuing education in the 1970s. For example, studies undertaken in the 1950s are today, for the most part, of only historical interest, useful mainly for purposes of comparison. Few of these, therefore, have been listed here. Because statements of opinion on women's education are so numerous, certain readers may note the absence of some that are fairly recent; those listed were chosen to provide a sampling of the range of opinion. The major criterion for selection of the modest number of references to material on educational behaviors and aspirations of high school students was pertinence to women's education beyond high school.

Items in the section on women's status, and in the section on basic research regarding women's social and cultural roles, feminine psychology and development, and sex differences in intellectual characteristics and academic performance, were deemed most representative and most likely to lead the reader to other sources.

Selections for the section on women and employment were made with an eye on the need to provide references regarding varied areas of employment as well as the employment of women of diverse demographic characteristics.

Bibliographies covering areas of interest related to women's education vary in quality of organization and in the standards exercised in selection of items. The variety of those included in this booklet reflects our desire to provide access to as wide as possible a range of materials.

The problem of classifying references is never easily resolved. Many references contain material pertinent to more than one classification. In such cases, we have listed the item under the heading to which it seemed *most* pertinent. A very few items are listed under more than one heading.

The primary function of annotation is to give readers information that will enable them to know how germane given works are to their interests. Annotations provide a guide to reading but are no substitute for it. So annotation, like compilation, involves a process of selection, especially in the case of longer works. Generally speaking, annotations in this booklet, when they do not refer to the total content of a work, refer to the aspect or aspects of a work that are most pertinent to the major focus of this bibliography. With few exceptions, these annotations do not evaluate a book or article. Inclusion of an item in the bibliography indicates that in the view of those responsible for selection it has significance. (Exclusion does *not*, as already noted, indicate the converse.)

Almost all items listed here are accessible through the usual library facilities of college or universities, or comparable sources. Items not readily available have usually been omitted, sometimes reluctantly. These include unpublished doctoral dissertations, largely because the task of making a fair and representative selection was beyond the scope of this undertaking.

A bibliographer's work is never complete. Valuable items may elude the most careful search or be excluded because they are impossible to procure. New materials are constantly appearing. In the behavioral sciences social issues and scientific inquiry are interrelated, and the last word is never in on either. Social issues are the outcome of changing social conditions that create new problems for people; scientific inquiries are generated by questions about human behavior and human circumstances to which such problems give rise.

The contents of this bibliography are ample evidence that the last appraisal of women's higher and continuing education is not in, nor the last bit of knowledge pertinent to such appraisal. Quite a lot is known about the characteristics of today's college women and something about those of women students in continuing education, but these characteristics are constantly changing with changing social conditions within and without the province of education. Much less is known about the range of uses to which women's education is put and how education determines these uses. Partly because we do not know very much about what education does to and for women, there is very little agreement about what the structures, processes, and contents of that education should be for what women under what circumstances. This lack of agreement stems also from lack of agreement both about what women's status *is* in our society and about what it *should* be. How available statistics on labor force participation, participation in education, and so on are interpreted (and even what statistics are compiled) depends on values associated with perceptions of women's status. These values, together with insufficiently sophisticated techniques of inquiry and measurement, are also responsible for conflicting theories and findings about women's psychological development and about sex differences.

The body of knowledge from which this bibliography has been drawn will not be an integrated whole in the foreseeable future. It will continue to grow, it is hoped, in depth as well as in volume. We have been concerned that our work serve the purposes any useful bibliography should; that is, provide its readers with clues to future sources of information and ideas as well as to past and present ones. If the materials have been organized in a fashion helpful and meaningful to our readers, our methods of classification may provide the rudiments of a system for filing the additions readers will be making in the course of time. We wish you all happy hunting—the game is and will remain plentiful.

Esther Manning Westervelt
Executive Codirector of the National Coalition for Research
on Women's Education and Development

Goshen, New York, May 1971

Acknowledgments

Bibliographers always owe a large debt of gratitude to other bibliographers. The published bibliographies we found useful are listed in later pages. We must particularly acknowledge an unpublished bibliography prepared by Mrs. Margaret Comstock, with the support of the College Entrance Examination Board, when she was a staff member of the Institute for the Study of Human Problems at Stanford University. The present bibliography grew out of what was originally an assignment by the College Board to revise and edit Mrs. Comstock's work, which focused on the roles, participation in the labor force, and education of adult women. Plans for revision were dropped in favor of broader coverage, but the Comstock bibliography provided us with some very useful leads. Her annotations served as a helpful check of our own understanding in a number of cases; also, several appear herein in their original form or with only minor editorial changes.

We must also acknowledge the support and interest of Carole Leland, formerly Executive Associate for Curriculum, College Entrance Examination Board, and S. A. Kendrick, Executive Director of Research and Development, College Entrance Examination Board. They kept our spirits from flagging before the task was finished.

Esther Manning Westervelt
Deborah A. Fixter

July 1971

Key to Abbreviations Used

SES — socioeconomic status

SVIB — Strong Vocational Interest Blank

SVIB-M — Strong Vocational Interest Blank-Men

SVIB-W — Strong Vocational Interest Blank-Women

SAT — Scholastic Aptitude Test of the College Entrance Examination Board

TAT — Thematic Apperception Test

MMPI — Minnesota Multiphasic Personality Inventory

OPI — Omnibus Personality Inventory

GPA — grade-point average

AFDC — Aid For Dependent Children

LPI — Leadership Potential Inventory

CPI — California Psychological Inventory

WRL — Word Rating List

ACT — American College Testing Program tests

GATB — General Aptitude Test Battery

AAUW — American Association of University Women

1. Statements, Studies, and Documents Pertaining to Women's Status

"The American Woman." *Trans-Action,* 1970(Nov-Dec),8(1 and 2).
Entire issue devoted to the status of women today. Contains numerous articles of interest including: Joan Jordan, "Working Women and the Equal Rights Amendment"; Inge Powell Bell, "The Double Standard"; and Marijean Suelzle, "Women in Labor."

Ashley-Montagu, Montague Francis. *The Natural Superiority of Women.* New York: Macmillan, 1953. (Also, London: Collier Books, 1970.)
An anthropologist's views on the biological and cultural advantages enjoyed by women, such as greater longevity, more resistance to stress, fewer role discontinuities, and many others. Written for the lay reader.

Bernard, Jessie. *Women and The Public Interest: An Analysis of Policy and Protest.* Chicago: Aldine Publishing Company. In preparation.
Broad coverage of areas of public interest and analysis of the concept of public policy, what it is and is not, and what women can and should do to effect public policy toward achievement of their own goals. (From publisher's abstract.)

Bird, Caroline, with Briller, Sarah Wells. *Born Female: The High Cost of Keeping Women Down.* New York: David McKay, 1968.
A detailed examination of discrimination against women in employment (salaries, pension plans, and so forth), based on other published studies, on statistical summaries, and on interviews with working women and social and business leaders. The author argues that "30 million working American women have been trained to accept inferior status, unequal pay for equal work, and penalties for getting pregnant and having children; to disclaim personal ambition; and to apologize for intellect and ability." The final chapter suggests needed changes in marriage, men's attitudes, and employment practices.

de Beauvoir, Simone. *The Second Sex.* Translated and edited by H. M. Parshley. New York: Knopf, 1953.
A classic statement on women's inferior position in society; the author draws on biology, psychology, literature, mythology, sociology and economics to document her thesis.

Discrimination against Women. Hearings before the Special Subcommittee of the Committee on Education and Labor, House of Representatives, Ninety-first Congress, Second Session on Section 805 of H.R. 16098. Hearings Held in Washington June 17, 19, and 30, 1970 (Part I) and July 1 and 31, 1970 (Part II). Washington, D.C.: Government Printing Office, 1970.

Of inestimable value in the assessment of the current status of women in education and employment. Contains reports on discrimination against women from an extremely wide variety of qualified sources.

Ellman, Mary. *Thinking about Women.* **New York: Harcourt, Brace & World, 1968.**
A feminist critic's analysis of the characterization and roles of women in literature and of the social and psychological sources of writers' perceptions.

Firestone, Shulamith. *The Dialectic of Sex: The Case for Feminist Revolution.* **New York: Morrow, 1970.**
An impassioned statement of the radical feminist position.

Flexner, Eleanor. *Century of Struggle: The Woman's Rights Movement in the United States.* **Cambridge, Massachusetts: The Belknap Press of Harvard University Press, 1959.**
Scholarly history of American women's battles for equal rights from 1800 through the ratification of the Nineteenth Amendment in 1920.

Friedan, Betty. *The Feminine Mystique.* **New York: W. W. Norton, 1963.**
Examination of problems women face because of stereotyping of women's roles and characteristics, and plea for abolition of sex stereotyping.

Graduate Comment, **1969,12(1). Detroit, Mich.: Graduate Division of Wayne State University.**
Entire issue on women's status with emphasis on discrimination against career-oriented women. Specifically notes the fields of publishing, medicine, higher education, and architecture.

Greer, Germaine. *The Female Eunuch.* **New York: McGraw-Hill, 1971.**
A cogent, literate statement of the radical feminist position. The author attacks cultural stereotypes of women, of femininity, of love, marriage and family life, and homosexuality. She contends that the polarity of masculine-feminine is not tenable under current and emerging cultural and social conditions but acknowledges that the abandonment of such a long held perspective is difficult and frightening. The author grew up in Australia and is now an English citizen but appears to be speaking for feminists of all nationalities. The author's style is light; the content mixes scholarly insights with narrative and personal observation.

Grimes, Alan P. *The Puritan Ethic and Woman Suffrage.* **New York: Oxford University Press, 1967.**
An interesting historical analysis of conservative sources of support for woman suffrage.

Kanowitz, Leo. *Women and the Law: The Unfinished Revolution.* **Albuquerque: University of New Mexico Press, 1969.**
The author covers the legal aspects of employment, rape, abortion, prostitu-

tion and divorce; the rights of single and of married women; draws the female/black parallel.

Kraditor, Aileen S., ed. *Up from the Pedestal: Selected Writings in the History of American Feminism.* **Chicago: Quadrangle, 1968.**
Anthology of documents selected from the feminist literature of the mid-nineteenth through mid-twentieth centuries. Illustrative of the earliest questioning of women's place in American society and the opposition to it, the emergence of specific areas of discontent, the suffrage movement, and current efforts to effect full equality for women.

Kresge, Pat. "**The Human Dimensions of Sex Discrimination.**" AAUW *Journal*, 1970(Nov),64(2),6-9.
Nearly 8,000 AAUW questionnaire responses indicate the greatest discrimination against women occurs in the South and in the 50-59 age group. A "mosaic" of case histories correspondents submitted as supplements to the questionnaire is presented.

Millett, Kate. *Sexual Politics.* **New York: Doubleday, 1970.**
Analysis of the influence of sexism in the behavioral sciences and literature and of the pervasiveness of a patriarchal model in social and political arrangements.

Morgan, Robin, ed. *Sisterhood Is Powerful: An Anthology of Writings from the Women's Liberation Movement.* **New York: Vintage Books, Random House, 1970.**
Articles, poems, photographs, and manifestos, contributed by more than 50 women, reflect the abuse of women in the major institutions of our society and the wide range of political theory and action in the women's liberation movement.

Morgan, Robin, ed. *Women in Revolt*, **New York: Random House, 1969.**
Anthology of feminists' writings covering a wide range and drawn in large part from "On the Liberation of Women," a special double issue of *Motive*, 1969 (Mar-Apr),29(6 and 7).

O'Neill, William L. *Everyone Was Brave: The Rise and Fall of Feminism in America.* **Chicago: Quadrangle, 1969.**
History of feminism in America from about 1830 to about 1850. Good coverage of the "old" feminism; no coverage of the "new."

Painter, Edith G. "**Women: The Last of the Discriminated.**" *Journal of the National Association of Women Deans and Counselors*, 1971(Winter), 34(2),59-62.
Probes the fallacy of progress in women's rights, indicating actual decline in women's financial, political, and academic statuses, and suggests that solutions to inequalities lie not in militancy but in educational and governmental

resources and in the responsibility of women themselves to educate the younger female generations.

Presidential Task Force on Women's Rights and Responsibilities, Virginia R. Allan, chairman. *A Matter of Simple Justice.* **Washington, D.C.: Government Printing Office, 1969.**
Set of recommendations for improving women's status based on carefully collected data regarding women's status in relation to equal employment and manpower training opportunities, equal access to opportunities in public education, discrimination in public accommodations, equal pay, social security benefits, child care aid and services, federal employee fringe benefits, income tax revisions. Includes among its recommendations establishment of a White House Office of Women's Rights and Responsibilities whose female director should also serve as Special Assistant to the President.

"Revolution II: Thinking Female." *College and University Business,* **1970(Feb),51-86.**
This section of the publication offers a sampling of articles dealing with discrimination (Rossi), education (Buccieri), and additional areas of female deprivation.

Rossi, Alice. "Sex Equality: The Beginning of Ideology." *The Humanist,* **1969(Sep-Oct),29(5),3-6,16.**
Explores aspects of discrimination effected by sexual, as contrasted with racial or religious, inequality. Examines possibilities for feminine equality in pluralist, assimilation, and hybrid models of society. In the last, the author perceives the only chance for true equality for women.

Scott, Anne Firor, ed. *The American Woman: Who Was She?* **Englewood Cliffs, N. J.: Prentice-Hall, 1971.**
Selection of articles and reports, by men and women, documenting developments, from the midnineteenth century to the present, occasioned by the changing role of women in American society, in women's education, work, participation in reform movements, and views of family life.

Scott, Anne Firor. *The Southern Lady: From Pedestal to Politics.* **Chicago: University of Chicago Press, 1970.**
Carefully documented history of the changing status and widening sphere of influence of the Southern woman from antebellum days to 1930. The most comprehensive treatment of this subject currently available.

Scott, Anne Firor, ed. *What Is Happening to American Women.* **Atlanta, Ga.: Southern Newspapers Publishers Association Foundation, 1970.**
Proceedings of a seminar for Southern journalists to illuminate social, cultural, and economic realities behind the rising surge of feminism. Includes: Anne Firor Scott, "Where We Have Been and Where We Are Going"; Bruno Bettelheim, "The Change in Woman's Role in Home and Society"; Joy D.

Osofsky, "The Socialization and Education of American Females"; Joyce A. Landner, "Women in Poverty: Its Roots and Effects"; Esther M. Westervelt, "Education, Vocation and Avocation in Women's Lives"; Catherine East, "What Do Women Want?"; and Marlene D. Dixon, "The New Woman's Movement."

Tanner, Leslie B. *Voices from Women's Liberation.* **New York: Signet Book Division, New American Library, 1970.**
Collection of writings by women of the past and present equal rights movements. Extensive coverage of militant feminists of the past. Views of current liberationists on a wide range of issues and aspects of the present movement.

U. S. Department of Labor, Wage and Standards Administration, Women's Bureau. *American Women.* **Report of the President's Commission on the Status of Women. Washington, D.C.: Government Printing Office, 1963.**
Data and recommendations on diverse aspects of the lives of American women: education and counseling; home and community; women in employment; labor standards; security of basic income; status under the law; and women as citizens.

Westervelt, Esther M. "From Evolution to Revolution" (6-9) and "From Evolution to Revolution II" (10-14), in *An Imperative for the Seventies: Releasing Creative Woman Power.* **A Guide for Counselors of Mature Women. St. Louis, Mo.: University of Missouri at St. Louis, Extension Division, 1969.**
Challenging the slow pace of cultural evolution, the author outlines the need for revolution in areas such as women's higher education and in present perceptions of the role of the nuclear family in today's society.

"What to Do about Discrimination." AAUW *Journal,* **1970(Nov),10-13.**
Panel of four female representatives from politics, psychology, psychiatry, and law suggest 12 ways to combat various forms of sex discrimination.

"The Woman in America." *Daedalus,* **1964(Spring),93(2).**
Thoughtful, scholarly essays by Erikson, Rossi, Peterson, Degler, and others. Many still timely.

"Women around the World." *Annals of the American Academy of Political and Social Science,* **1968(Jan),375.**
Entire issue contains numerous articles of interest including: Jessie Bernard, "The Status of Women in Modern Patterns of Culture"; Jeanne Clare Ridley, "Demographic Change and the Roles and Status of Women."

"Women in Transition." AAUW *Journal,* **1970(Nov),64(2),2-26.**
Articles on aspects of current endeavors to ameliorate the status of women: Pat Kresge, "The Human Dimensions of Sex Discrimination"; Ruth M. Oltman, "Campus 1970 — Where Do Women Stand?"; John B. Parrish, "Coming

Crisis in Women's Higher Education and Work"; Esther M. Westervelt, "Are We Ready for Equality?"; and Alice L. Beeman and Shirley McCune, "Changing Styles of Volunteer Organizations."

2. Statements on the Education of Women

Cless, Elizabeth L. "A Modest Proposal for the Educating of Women."
  The American Scholar, 1969(Autumn),38(4),618-627.
Attacking the fallacy of equality for women in the present male-oriented educational structure, the author urges greater procedural flexibilities in education to accommodate the variety of female life patterns.

David, Opal D. *The Education of Women: Signs for the Future.* Report
  of a Conference on the Present Status and Prospective Trends of Research on the Education of Women. Washington, D.C.: American Council on Education, 1959.
Of historical interest.

Frank, Lawrence K. "A Plea for an Education for Women." *Vassar Alumnae Magazine*, 1961(May),1ff.
A discussion of the special relevance for women of contemporary teaching methods that draw upon intuitive as well as analytical thought processes, such as learning by discovery.

Froomkin, Joseph. *Aspirations, Enrollments, and Resources: The Challenge to Higher Education in the Seventies.* U. S. Office of Education.
  Washington, D.C.: Government Printing Office, 1970.
Data on sex differences in the indicated areas.

Heist, Paul. "A Commentary on the Motivation and Education of College
  Women." *Journal of the National Association of Women Deans and Counselors*, 1962(Jan),25(2),51-59.
The author reviews changes in sex-roles, the educational status of women, and the increasing need for women in the labor force. Although women in general are found to score the same or better than men on measures of interest in ideas and abstract thought, attitude scales and on the SVIB-M intellectual categories, women almost without exception look ahead to marriage, with education or employment as only temporary interests. The author suggests that stereotypes of female roles continuously mitigate against strong vocational, academic and professional commitments and that neither the home nor previous schooling has given genuine value to the learning process.

Jencks, Christopher and David Riesman. *The Academic Revolution.* Garden City, N.Y.: Anchor Books, Doubleday, 1969, Chapter VII.
The book is a sociological and historical analysis of American higher education. Chapter VII reviews the rise of coeducational and women's colleges. The authors evaluate the past and future relationship of women's education to women's needs and predict a declining influence of women's colleges on educational trends.

McGuigan, Dorothy Gies. *A Dangerous Experiment: 100 Years of Women at The University of Michigan*. Ann Arbor, Mich.: Center for Continuing Education for Women, University of Michigan, 1970.
Story of women's struggle to gain admission to the University and to attain equal opportunities and recognition, of ways in which the first graduates used their education, and of the status achieved by women within the century.

Mueller, Kate Hevner. *Educating Women for a Changing World*. Minneapolis: University of Minnesota Press, 1954.
Presentation of a philosophy on and a basic program for women's education which advocates an infinite variety of educational patterns designed to contribute most fully to a woman's personal development in all phases of her activity (work, home, community, nation) and to facilitate her adjustment to changing social roles.

Newcomer, Mabel. *A Century of Higher Education for Women*. New York: Harper & Bros., 1959.
A history of women's higher education in America from its beginnings in the nineteenth century through the mid-1950s. Well documented and the most comprehensive treatment of the subject presently available.

President's Commission on the Status of Women. *Report of the Committee on Education*. Washington, D.C.: Government Printing Office, 1963.
Study concerns the educational needs of all American women in all aspects. For the mature woman: elementary and secondary education; continuing education and financial support; continuance of continuing education at home. For the school and college student: basic educational quality and improvement of educational opportunities equally accessible to all; guidance and counseling; education for the home; accessible to all; guidance and counseling; education for the home, health, and family; education for volunteer activities; and research on the education of women. Extensive selected bibliography on women's education and interests was prepared for the report by the Radcliffe Institute.

Rush, Benjamin. *Of the Mode of Education Proper in a Republic*. Philadelphia, 1786.
A recommendation that women's education be broadened with the rationale that some education in moral philosophy, history, literature, and the sciences would prepare girls to participate more fully in the education of their sons and be more worthy companions for their husbands in lonely colonial homes. Of considerable historical interest.

Simpson, Alan. "A Livable Environment: The Educated Woman's Responsibility." *Journal of the National Association of Women Deans and Counselors*, 1966(Summer),39(4),147-149.
A plea for the place of conservation courses on women's curriculums and the

educated woman's commitment to the improvement of urban and rural environment.

U. S. Department of Labor, Wage and Standards Administration, Women's Bureau. *Trends in the Educational Attainment of Women.* **Washington, D.C.: Government Printing Office, 1967.**
Inclusive survey defining directions of women's education and presenting implications for these trends.

White, Lynn Townsend. *Educating Our Daughters: A Challenge to the Colleges.* **New York: Harper, 1950.**
Proposal for women's undergraduate education to include curricular and co-curricular offerings in traditional "feminine" activities (for example, flower arranging).

Whitney, Mary E. "The Struggle to Attain Coeducation." *Journal of the National Association of Women Deans and Counselors,* **1970(Fall),34(1), 38-44.**
Legal and academic history of women's struggle to gain admission to the University of Virginia, founded in 1819; traces obstacles and setbacks from 1879 through 1970 when women finally gained full admission status and the opportunity to earn the bachelor's degree.

"Women 16 to 60: Education for Full Maturity." *Journal of the National Association of Women Deans and Counselors,* **1966(Summer),29(4).**
Collection of writings on campus problems and programs and life phases as students, individuals, and employees makes up this entire issue devoted to women's education.

Woody, Thomas H. *A History of Women's Education in the United States.* **New York: Octagon Press, 1966. (c. 1929)**
Of historical interest.

3. Basic Research Relevant to Women's Education

A. Theories and Research on Women's Social and Cultural Roles

Dahlstrom, Edmund, ed. *The Changing Roles of Men and Women.* Translated by Gunilla and Steven Anderman. London: Gerald Duckworth & Co., Ltd., 1967.
Report of research on Scandinavian sex roles and effects of sex role changes on men and, especially, women as employees and as parents and on the child's personality development.

D'Andrade, Roy G. "Sex Differences and Cultural Institutions," in Maccoby, Eleanor E., ed., *The Development of Sex Differences.* Stanford, Calif.: Stanford University Press, 1966, pp. 173-204.
Review of ways in which sex differences have been culturally institutionalized.

Dornbusch, Sanford M. "Afterword," in Maccoby, Eleanor E., ed., *The Development of Sex Differences*, pp. 205-219.
Synthesis of papers in the text, written from the point of view of a sociologist.

Freedman, Mervin B. "The Role of the Educated Woman: Attitudes of Vassar Students" (Chapter 9) and "Women and Work" (Chapter 10), in Mervin Freedman, *The College Experience.* San Francisco: Jossey Bass, 1967.
Findings from a study of 49 Vassar students tested and interviewed during the four years of college. Students did not value feminine characteristics and behaviors but most aspired to marriage; the majority (69 percent) also wanted a career. Career-oriented students were more intellectual, unconventional, independent, and flexible in thinking and outlook and less traditional and authoritarian in attitudes than those not career oriented. Students were optimistic about being able to manage marriage and career and not concerned with feminist issues (these students were in college in the late 1950s): most of them expect that they would encounter more difficulties than men in pursuing careers, mainly because of the need to manage both domestic and career roles.

Mead, Margaret. *Male and Female: A Study of the Sexes in a Changing World.* New York: William Morrow & Co., 1953.
Cross-cultural study of the sexes; discussion of sex, temperament, and development and the effects on these of societal conditions. Major section is devoted to sex-identity development, behavior, and needs of men and women in contemporary American culture.

Myrdal, Alva, and Klein, Viola. *Women's Two Roles: Work and Home.* London: Routledge and Kegan Paul, 1956.

Analysis and discussion of the home-career dichotomy often postulated for women, and trends in its resolution in England, France, Sweden, and America.

Rossi, Alice. "Ambivalence in Women: Should We Plan for the Real or the Ideal?" *Adult Leadership.* **1967(Sep),16(3),100-102,118.**

Continuing education programs for women run the risk of instilling in women who are ambivalent about work roles the notion that careful career planning and professional commitment are not necessary since retraining and reorientation through continuing education programs are available. Women's ambivalence toward their major social roles is a function of these factors: (1) there is no social role toward which there is no ambivalence; (2) roles vary in the extent to which it is culturally and psychologically permissible to express ambivalence; (3) ambivalence can be admitted most readily toward those roles which are optional; and (4) the more critical the role is for the maintenance and survival of a society, the greater the likelihood that the negative side of ambivalence will be repressed and negative sanctions applied to its expression. Thus it is as socially unacceptable for men to show negative attitudes toward work as it is for women to show negative attitudes toward marriage and maternity. The masculine tone of American society and the high primacy given to individuality are important roots of ambivalence in women; these aspects of our society have implications for the maternal role and make the employment concept less attractive to women. The trend toward the elimination of cooperation in our society needs to be reversed to free both men and women from the confinement of sex-role constrictions and conflicts.

Seeley, John; Sim, R. A.; and Loosley, E. W. *Crestwood Heights: A Study of the Culture of Suburban Life.* **New York: Basic Books, 1956. Chapter 12.**

Sociopsychological analysis of the differences in beliefs and life styles of men and women in the suburban community studied by this interdisciplinary team. Although the suburb was in Canada and the study completed some years ago, observations of American suburbs seem to support the analysis.

Steinmann, Anne. "A Study of the Concept of the Feminine Role of 51 Middle-Class American Families." *Genetic Psychology Monographs,* **1963, 67(2),275-352.**

In viewing the feminine role, both mothers and daughters agreed that (a) it consists in equal degrees of traditional (other-oriented) and liberal (self-oriented) elements; (b) self-concepts and ideal concepts are closely related; (c) their concepts of the average woman's and the man's ideal woman are more other-oriented than their own ideal woman; (d) men's ideal woman is more other-oriented than their own ideal woman and that of the average woman. Mothers view themselves as closer to the average woman than do their daughters. The father's ideal woman is seen as more other-oriented than is actually the case.

Steinmann, Anne. "Female-Role Perception as a Factor in Counseling."
Journal of the National Association of Women Deans and Counselors,
1970(Fall),34(1),27-33.

Responses to three forms of the Inventory of Feminine Values from 51 young
women (ages 17 to 22, unmarried) enrolled in a liberal arts college sociology
course indicated, for the most part, that the notions held by these women
were compatible with their parents' (who were interviewed) on the same
issues. In general, the young women did not think work was very important;
35 said they might work after graduation and of these, 20 said only if it was
financially necessary. Young women who do choose to go on to paid employment seem to reflect unfulfilled desires of their mothers. Fathers' views were
found to be a significant influence on student views. Since all the subjects had
high employment potential, the author suggests the need of a more clearly
defined role perception in order to eliminate family/employment conflict and
allow students the chance to assess their own needs.

Steinmann, Anne, and Fox, David J. "Male-Female Perceptions of the
Female Role in the United States." *Journal of Psychology,* 1966,42(2),
265-276.

Three forms of the Inventory of Feminine Values were administered to 562
men. (Compare Steinmann study below.) Data indicates that men's actual
ideal woman is not significantly different from women's own ideal or self-
perception. The men's ideal woman is thus significantly more active and self-
assertive than the ideal that women attributed to them.

Steinmann, Anne; Levi, J.; and Fox, David J. "Self-Concept of College
Woman Compared with Their Concept of Ideal Woman and Man's Ideal
Woman." *Journal of Counseling Psychology,* 1964(Winter),11(4),370-
374.

Three forms of the Inventory of Feminine Values were administered to 75
women attending a large metropolitan college. Data indicate that the women
perceived themselves and their ideal woman as essentially alike with equal
components of passive and active orientations; but they perceive man's ideal
woman as significantly more passive and accepting of a subordinate role in
both personality development and place in the family structure.

Westervelt, Esther Manning. "Woman as a Compleat Human Being."
Journal of The National Association of Women Deans and Counselors,
1966(Summer),29(4),150-155.

Women's traditional social roles in the home are of decreasing social significance and participation in the public domain is becoming an increasingly important route to self-fulfillment for women as well as for men. But the public
domain has been masculinized; employment patterns of hiring and advancement are derived from masculine life patterns and masculine qualities (for
example, aggressiveness, competitiveness, dominance) are those most highly
rewarded. The devaluing of feminine qualities (for example, nurturance, con-

cern with interpersonal relations, interest in maintaining order and stability) in the public domain restricts women's opportunity for self-fulfillment. Girls should be encouraged to enter careers because they are women (not in spite of the fact); in many careers (for example, in law, city management, medicine, architecture, and so forth) "feminine" qualities can serve both personal and social advantage.

Wilson, Kenneth. *Report to Member Colleges*. Princeton, N. J.: College Research Center, Educational Testing Service, 1971.
Of particular interest, among other findings, is one indicating increasing perception among female freshmen of women's roles as less traditional and more liberal in respect to occupational equality.

B. Theories and Research on Feminine Psychology and Development

Bardwick, Judith M. *Psychology of Women: A Study of Bio-Cultural Conflicts*. New York: Harper and Row, 1971.
Extensive physiological and psychological data on sex differences are used by the author to emphasize the genetic origins of certain sex differences and their implications for sex differences in social roles. Almost half of the book (98 out of 218 pages) is devoted to a discussion of the physiological bases of sex differences. The author states that in her opinion "differences between men and women originate interactively; in genetic temperamental differences, in differences in the adult reproductive system, and in sex-linked values specific to each culture." In her opinion, sex differences mandate the fundamental importance of marital and maternal roles to women's development, ego-strength, and self-esteem. The book does *not* draw on anthropological and biological sources to raise questions about the possible links between long-term cultural change and change in basic patterns of sex differences.

Brim, Orville G. Jr.; Glass, David C.; Lavin, David E.; and Goodman, Norman. *Personality and Decision Process: Studies in the Social Psychology of Thinking*. Stanford, Calif.: Stanford University Press, 1962.
Analysis of effects of personality, social characteristics and situational variables on the decision-making process. Chapter 3 includes discussion of differences as a parameter in the study; Chapter 7 reports findings on these. For middle-class but not for lower-class subjects, correlations were found for 9 similar characteristics (for example, intelligence) and for 17 dissimilar characteristics (for example, manifest anxiety in husbands and pessimism in wives). In the middle class, no sex differences on mean scores for any of the decision variables were found; among the lower class, women were more present-oriented than their husbands—in this respect, lower-class women differed from all other subjects. Lower-class males resembled the middle class in decision making but, like their wives, were low in autonomy compared to the middle class.

Clarkson, Frank E.; Vogel, Susan R.; Broverman, Inge K.; Broverman, Donald M.; and Rosenkrantz, Paul S. "Family Size and Sex-Role Stereotypes." *Science*, 1970 (Jan 23), 167,390-392.
Study of 96 Catholic mothers conducted to investigate relationships between completed family size and the self-concepts of women with respect to masculine-feminine traits. Results indicate that women who perceive themselves as possessing to a greater degree socially desirable masculine traits have fewer children than women who perceive themselves as more stereotypically feminine. The authors point out that it is difficult to determine if self-concept or family size is the cause or effect of this relationship and also suggest that an examination of these variables in non-Catholic women would supplement the findings of this report.

Cope, Robert G. "Sex-Related Factors and Attrition among College Women." *Journal of the National Association of Women Deans and Counselors*, 1970(Spring),33(3),118-124.
Report of a study which indicates that females who appear to lack personal attractiveness, esthetic inclinations, and verbal skill tend to withdraw from college.

Denmark, Florence L., and Guttentag, Marcia. "Dissonance in the Self-Concepts and Educational Concepts of College- and Non-College-Oriented Women." *Journal of Counseling Psychology*, 1967(Mar),14(2), 113-115.
Semantic differential techniques were used to evaluate the self and educational concepts of three groups of mature women differing in commitment and pursuit of college goals. Findings showed a positive relationship between the level of educational involvement and evaluation of educational activities and less discrepancy between present and ideal self-concepts.

Douvan, Elizabeth, and Gold, M. "Modal Patterns in American Adolescence," in Hoffman, Martin L., and Hoffman, Lois Wladis, eds., *Review of Child Development*. New York: Russell Sage Foundation, Volume II, 1966, pp. 469-528.
Review of research on adolescent development and educational behaviors during the secondary school years with ample coverage of sex differences. Excellent bibliography.

Dua, Prem S. "Personality Characteristics Differentiating Women Leaders from Non-Leaders in a University." *Journal of the National Association of Women Deans and Counselors*, 1964(Spring),27(2),128-132.
Research instruments included the Leadership Potential Inventory constructed specifically for this study. Employing a multiple regression analysis (64 variables, 52 of which came from the LPI) of data from two samples of 46 elected leaders and 46 nonleaders each, the author found support for the hypothesis that certain personal and social characteristics account for the

variance in elected leadership among college women. Dominance, Theoretical Value, and Acceptance (of the leadership role) appeared to be those characteristics especially predictive of leadership potential.

Farber, Seymour M., and Wilson, Roger H. L., eds. *The Potential of Woman.* **New York: McGraw-Hill, 1963.**
Essays on such topics as research findings concerning female nonhuman primates, biological makeup of women; research on differences in intellect between men and women, boys and girls; differences in psychosexual development; cultivation of female qualities in men; implications of equality between men and women; forms of rivalry between men and women; the emancipation movement of the nineteenth and early twentieth centuries, and its present status; women's roles; women as patrons of the arts; women as investors; problems of creative women.

Goldberg, Philip. "Are Women Prejudiced against Women?" *Trans-Action,* **1968(Apr),5(5),28-30.**
In evaluating articles arbitrarily attributed to male and female authors, regardless of the actual sex of the author, college women consistently gave higher ratings to those purportedly written by men, even in the case of articles dealing with traditional "female" occupations.

Gough, Harrison C. "College Attendance among High School Students as Predicted from the California Psychological Inventory." *Journal of Counseling Psychology,* **1968(May),15(3),269-278.**
In this study designed to attempt to identify the predictors of dropout potential among high school high-aptitude students (one third to one half do not go on to college), the CPI, Intellectual Ability, and Scholastic Achievement measures were used on 220 high-aptitude students from 9 schools and 212 high-aptitude students and 899 randomly selected students from 8 additional schools. Predictive validities of .51 and .37 were obtained for high-aptitude male and female students, respectively; for male and female unselected students, .51 and .52. Findings noted that family, income, sex, and scholastic attainment are relevant but not compelling factors regarding college attendance. Males who were rational, mature, ambitious, and capable, and females who were dominant, logical, determined, and aggressive were found to be those most likely to attend college. There was a low correlation between college attendance and apathy, shiftlessness, confusion, and mischievousness among male high-aptitude students, and gentleness, affection, timidity, and meekness among female high-aptitude students.

Horner, Matina S. "Women's Will to Fail." *Psychology Today,* **1969(Mar), 3(6),36-38.**
Women's achievement motivation is shown by this study to be detrimentally influenced by sex differentials acquired through socialization.

Horney, Karen. *Feminine Psychology.* Kelman, Harold, ed. New York: Norton, 1967.

A collection of Horney's essays on the psychology of women. (Horney was among the earliest to question some of Freud's theories on women.)

Kagan, Jerome. "Acquisition and Significance of Sex Typing and Sex Role Identity," in Hoffman and Hoffman, eds., *Review of Child Development.* New York: Russell Sage Foundation, Volume I, 1964, pp. 137-168.

Effects of socialization, including educational practices, on the development of sex differences (including academic), role preferences, and aspirations. Excellent bibliography.

Lehman, Irving J.; Sinha, Birendra K.; and Hartnett, Rodney T. "Changes in Attitudes and Values Associated with College Attendance." *Journal of Educational Psychology,* 1966(Apr),57(3),89-98.

In 1958 a battery of instruments was administered to 1,747 college freshmen and administered again four years later whether or not the subjects were still attending college. Findings noted that, regardless of sex and length of college attendance, the subjects became less stereotypic in their beliefs, less dogmatic, and more "outer directed" in their value orientation; there appeared no significant relationship between general academic aptitude and either degree or direction of changes. Female subjects, regardless of time spent in college, appeared to undergo more marked changes in attitudes and values than did their male counterparts over the four-year period.

Lewis, Edwin C. *Developing Women's Potential.* Ames, Iowa: University of Iowa Press, 1968.

Wide-ranging review of research pertinent to women's development and education. Excellent bibliography.

Rosenberg, B. G., and Sutton-Smith, B. "Family Interaction Effects on Masculinity-Femininity." *Journal of Personality and Social Psychology,* 1968(Feb),8(2),117-120.

160 two-child families were studied to assess parental and sibling variables on masculinity-femininity. 160 college sophomores and their families were given the Gough Scale of Psychological Femininity. Results indicate that effects of sibling-sibling, child-parent, and parent-child relationships are factors in sex role preference. Sibling's status appears to be related to sex-role preference; girls with brothers tend to respond to relative isolation by identifying more strongly with the mother; fathers with two female children scored higher on masculinity than when one of the children was male.

Sanford, Nevitt. *Self and Society.* New York: Atherton Press, 1966. Chapters 12 and 16.

Chapter 12 (Masculinity-Femininity in the Structure of Personality) presents a developmental model intended to guide work of social institutions that mold the individual's personality in order for the structural processes that occur in college to promote more mature self-concepts in the area of masculinity-femininity. Chapter 16 (Changing Sex Roles, Socialization, and Education) sketches the sex role spheres in the United States and, basing inquiries on studies of Vassar students, discusses how young women achieve sex identity and adapt to changing requirements of women's roles while seeking to attain wholeness as an individual.

Simon, William, and Gagnon, John. "Psychosexual Development." *Trans-Action*, 1969(Mar),6(5),9-17.
A discussion of male and female psychosexual development from childhood, through adolescence, to adulthood; in instances, development related to socioeconomic status, educational achievement, personal characteristics and motivation. Authors suggest that success for women in higher education and the professions is because of aggression and/or deviancy but attribute these factors to sociological rather than biological influences.

Tukey, Ruth S. "Intellectually-Oriented and Socially-Oriented Superior College Girls." *Journal of the National Association of Women Deans and Counselors*, 1964(Spring),27(3),120-127.
23 college juniors and seniors who qualified as socially-oriented subjects (held 4 positions of campus leadership) and 25 who qualified as intellectually-oriented (minimum of 135 IQ and absence of record of leadership in important campus organizations) were asked to respond to the Edwards Personal Preference Schedule and the Rokeach Test for Dogmatism in an effort to determine why some superior girls chose the social role while others the intellectual role. For each group, the mean GPA was 3.48. Significant measured differences are noted: the intellectually oriented girls have a greater need for achievement and autonomy, while the socially oriented girls possess a greater need for expressing deference. Their needs for heterosexual relationships appeared similar, although occupational aspirations and goals seemed to be influenced by the interpretation of how this need was to be met. Socially oriented girls also appeared bound by conformity and thus do not achieve their potential.

Winborn, Bob B., and Jansen, David G. "Personality Characteristics of Campus Social-Political Action Leaders." *Journal of Counseling Psychology*, 1967(Nov),14(6),509-513.
90 percent of the men and 96 percent of the women in the total selected sample group of 257 student leaders participated in this 1966 study of social-political action leaders, religious organization leaders, residence hall leaders, activities leaders, and fraternity leaders. All participants completed Form A of the 16 Personality Factor Questionnaire and findings indicate that the social-political leaders differed from the other leaders primarily in Superego Strength, Autia, and Radicalism. The sex of the leader did not appear to be a significant influence on isolating these three factors, nor did sex seem a sig-

nificant variable in distinguishing social-political leaders from other group leaders.

C. Theories and Research on Sex Differences in Intellectual Characteristics and Academic Performance

Astin, Alexander. *The College Environment*. Washington, D.C.: American Council on Education, 1968.
With data based on 30,570 questionnaire responses from students who had completed their freshman year in 246 institutions (accredited four-year colleges or universities), the author attempted to identify distinguishing characteristics and to measure their effect on different types of college environments. The Inventory of College Activities was administered and analyzed in relation to peer environment, classroom environment, physical environment, administrative environment, and the college image as represented by athletics, competitiveness, school spirit, concern for individual, and so forth. These environmental phases are summarized by type of curriculum and control, geographic region, race, and sex.

Bayley, Nancy. "Behavioral Correlates of Mental Growth: Birth to Thirty-Six Years." *American Psychologist*, 1968(Jan),23(1),1-17.
Longitudinal records covering a 36-year life span for 54 subjects provide the data for this study which measures male and female cognitive processes. The author presents patterns of correlation between behaviors in the first three years and verbal scores over the 36-year span; prediction of girls' adult verbal scores from these behaviors is less tentative than that of boys' scores. Ratings of maternal behavior in the first three years correlated with children's behaviors and with children's intelligence through the first 18 years; sex differences in these patterns of correlations lead to the suggestion that there are genetically determined sex differences in that boys appear to be more permanently affected by the emotional climate in infancy than were girls. Other findings include: females' mental abilities stabilize at an earlier age, while males exhibit stability later; for girls, the Vocalization Precocity score at as young as 1 year correlates persistently with later verbal scores and reaches the peak point of correlation at 26 years; for girls there was revealed considerable independence of intelligence from personality variables (shyness is the only variable that can be shown to correlate even moderately with later intelligence); for females at ages 16 and 36, scores on the Digit Symbol test are independent of other factors on the mental scale and of behavior variables, again suggesting the possibility of genetic determiners of intelligence since for males, scores show less independence of verbal factors.

Broverman, Inge K.; Broverman, Donald M.; Clarkson, Frank E.; Rosenkrantz, Paul S.; and Vogel, Susan R. "Sex-Role Stereotypes and Clinical Judgements of Mental Health." *Journal of Consulting and Clinical*

Psychology, 1970(Feb),34(1),1-7.

Clinicians were the subject of this study. It was found that clinicians, when they know the sex of the subject, describe mental health in terms of sex stereotypes but that ideals for mental health for an adult of unspecified sex are judged by clinicians to be those behaviors that are judged as healthy for men and differ from the behaviors judged healthy for women.

Connell, David M., and Johnson, James E. "Relationship between Sex-Role Identification and Self Esteem in Early Adolescents." *Developmental Psychology*, 1970(Sep),3(2),268.

Results of the Gough Feminine Scale and the Coopersmith Self-Esteem Inventory administered to Catholic early adolescents indicate that greater value is placed in the male role and that sex-role behavior is more vulnerable to peer criticism than adult criticism.

Cummins, Emery J., and Lindblade, Zondra G. "Sex-Based Differences among Student Disciplinary Offenders." *Journal of Counseling Psychology*, 1967(Jan),14(1),81-85.

To test differences between male and female disciplinary offenders, the subjects (95 males and 49 females) were matched with nondisciplinary subjects on sex, academic ability, and socioeconomic status; all were administered four measures: Tests of Critical Thinking, Inventory of Beliefs, Form I; Differential Value Inventory; and Rokeach's Dogmatism Scale, Form E. Disciplinary males scored significantly higher than disciplinary females on the Rokeach and Differential Value Tests, indicating they hold more traditional values and are more dogmatic than disciplinary women. On the other two tests, there were no significant measured differences between disciplinary males and females. In the case of nondisciplinary males and females, the only significant difference appeared in the dogmatism scale; again the females showed less dogmatism.

Droege, Robert C. "Sex Difference in Aptitude Maturation during High School." *Journal of Counseling Psychology*, 1967(Sep),14(5),407-411.

20,541 students were given ability tests in grades 9, 10, 11 and then retested in grade 12; another group (6,167) were tested in grade 12 when the larger sample was initially tested in the lower grades. Test score comparisons indicate that aptitude increases attributed to maturation, as well as correlation between the initial and retest scores, were about the same for boys and girls.

Elkind, David. "Quantity Conceptions in College Students." *Journal of Social Psychology*, 1962(Aug),57(Pt.2),459-465.

153 female and 87 male psychology students participated in a series of experiments to assess their abstract conceptions of weight, mass, and volume and to compare results with previous experiments (Piaget) with elementary and secondary school students. The hypothesis being tested: that concept correctness increased with age and was found more in males than in females.

92 percent of the sample passed the weight and mass tests, but only 58 percent passed the volume test; of this latter group, 74 percent of the males but only 52 percent of the females were successful. Findings indicate that concept correctness correlated with age and that an increase in concept correctness was found for women but not for men.

French, Elizabeth G., and Lesser, Gerald S. "Some Characteristics of the Achievement Motivation in Women." *Journal of Abnormal and Social Psychology,* 1964(Feb),68(2),119-128.

72 female students from four colleges participated in this study of motivation based on figure-oriented essays. Motivation scores were higher in intellectual arousal when figures of males were used and higher in woman's role arousal when female figures were used. Findings suggest that women who are comfortable being women are free to achieve or not achieve.

Gallagher, James J. "Sex Differences in Expressive Thought of Gifted Children in the Classroom." *Personnel and Guidance Journal,* 1966 (Nov),45(3),248-253.

Based on a sample of 92 high achieving girls and 97 high achieving boys, test results show the boys to be more expressive in classroom situations; the boys had significantly more positive self-concepts than the girls in the study although the girls showed significantly more positive attitudes toward their family and toward other people than did the boys. Gifted girls appeared to be less expressive in the public domain of oral interchange but not in the private dimension of written interchange.

Green, Robert Lee, and Farquar, William W. "Negro Academic Motivation and Scholastic Achievement." *Journal of Educational Psychology,* 1965(Oct),56(5),241-243.

Sample subjects included 104 male Negroes and 129 female Negroes from the eleventh grades of two Detroit high schools representing a diversity of socio-economic levels and 254 Caucasian males and 261 Caucasian females from a total of 4,200 eleventh-graders in 9 Michigan high schools. Both racial groups were measured on academic motivation, verbal aptitude, and school achievement (GPA). These variables were correlated with sex and race. While aptitude and motivation were found to correlate significantly for Caucasian subjects of both sexes and for Negro women, for Negro males significant correlation occurred only between motivation and achievement. No correlation was found between aptitude and achievement for Negro males. The Word Rating List (self-concept measure in battery of instruments used to assess academic motivation) appeared to be the best indicator of achievement for the Negro sample; for white males, verbal aptitude; for white females, the WRL.

Hill, Arthur. "A Longitudinal Study of Attrition among High Aptitude

College Students." *Journal of Educational Research*, 1966(Dec),60(4), 166-173.

Sample was composed of 628 high aptitude freshmen (M-308, F-320) who participated in a summer 1959 orientation program and had graduated or had withdrawn from the University of Texas by the spring of 1964 and who responded to a follow-up questionnaire regarding reasons for leaving the university, current status, and future plans. Responses according to sex and graduate or withdrawal status were analyzed in relationship to age, high school graduation quartile, size of high school graduating class, father's occupation, student's vocational plans, and scores from a battery of tests including the SVIB, CPI, Gough, and the University of Texas Admissions and English Placement Tests. Of those who graduated, 179 were male, 194 female; of those who had withdrawn, 70 were male and 108 were female; of those who had been dismissed, 59 were male and 18 were female. Predominant reasons for voluntary withdrawal were "transfer" for males, "marriage" for females. Those who had been forced to withdraw gave superficial reasons for leaving the university. Findings also noted that among high aptitude students three times more boys than girls were dismissed for academic failure.

Laughlin, Patrick R.; Doherty, Mary A.; and Dunn, Ralph F. "Intentional and Incidental Concept Formation as a Function of Motivation, Creativity, Intelligence, and Sex." *Journal of Personality and Social Psychology*, 1968(Apr),8(4),401-409.

348 male and 348 female high school students were given an intentional concept-formation task as a cover for a later incidental concept-formation task; subjects were classified according to creativity and intelligence levels and both tasks were analyzed for creativity, motivation, and sex, with intelligence as covariate, and intelligence, motivation, and sex, with creativity as covariate. The authors found both types of concept formation increased directly as a function of both creativity and intelligence and that there was greater concept formation for males than females in both the intelligence and creativity groups. Findings also seemed to indicate that females were under a higher habitual motivational level as a personality state, and hence their performance was hindered by increased external motivation.

Laughlin, Patrick R.; McGlynn, Richard P.; Anderson, Jon A.; and Jacobson, Everett S. "Concept Attainment by Individuals Versus Cooperative Pairs as a Function of Memory, Sex, and Concept Rule." *Journal of Personality and Social Psychology*, 1968(Apr),8(4),410-417.

Individual and cooperative pair performances were compared on three successive concept attainment problems. Findings demonstrate the superiority of cooperative pair over individual problem-solving; males and females did not differ, which may indicate sufficient motivation for the females' performance to capacity; and also indicate that the effect of memory in concept learning applies relatively more to females than to males; and that males more than females profit from working with a partner.

Lesser, Gerald S.; Krawitz, Rhoda N.; and Packard, Rita. "Experimental Arousal of Achievement Motivation in Adolescent Girls." *Journal of Abnormal and Social Psychology,* **1963(Jan),66(1),59-66.**
40 female underachievers (mean IQ-131.86) and 40 female achievers (mean IQ-132.36) were selected from the junior and senior classes of a highly competitive high school representative of a middle-class population to participate in a study of the effect of arousal on achievement motivation. Under both Neutral and Achievement Orientation conditions, these groups were shown pictures with male(s) or female(s) as the leading figure(s). The achievement motivation of underachievers increased in Achievement Orientation conditions when pictures of males were shown; pictures of females produced greater motivation in achievers under the same conditions.

Leventhal, D. B.; Shemberg, K. M.; and Van Schoelandt, S. Kaye. "Effects of Sex-Role Adjustment upon the Expression of Aggression." *Journal of Personality and Social Psychology,* **1968(Apr),8(4),393-396.**
40 students, divided into four groups on the basis of masculinity test scores (low scoring males, high scoring males, low scoring females, high scoring females), were exposed to a situation demanding an aggressive response. The authors found that masculine males and feminine females express a greater degree of aggression than do their counterparts, that is, a marked tendency to aggress correlates with high sex-role adjustment.

Maccoby, Eleanor E., ed. *The Development of Sex Differences.* **Stanford, Calif.: Stanford University Press, 1966.**
Essays on biological, intellectual, psychosocial, social, and cultural aspects of the development of sex differences. See other references herein.

Maccoby, Eleanor E. "Sex Differences in Intellectual Functioning," in Maccoby, Eleanor E., ed., *The Development of Sex Differences.* **Stanford, Calif.: Stanford University Press, 1966, pp. 25-55.**
Review of findings regarding sex differences in average performance on ability tests covering general, verbal, number, spatial, and analytic intelligence; creativity; and achievement. Also presented are correlations between intellectual performance and personality characteristics (impulse control, fearfulness and anxiety, aggression and competitiveness, aspiration and achievement motivation levels, sex-typing, and dependency, passivity and independence). The author also discusses possible causal factors of sex differences in intellectual abilities (that is, genetic and environmental factors).

Magoon, Thomas M., and Maxwell, Martha J. "Demographic Differences between High and Low Achieving University Students." *Journal of College Student Personnel,* **1965(Nov),6(6),367-373.**
High achieving male and female students drawn from colleges of a university for this study responded to 22 demographic and attitudinal items on the Offi-

cial Student Information Survey as a part of fall registration; a contrasting group of low achievers was drawn from the same colleges and represented the same sex groupings. Results were analyzed to determine if demographic variables might differentiate between the two classes of achievers. Results indicated that eight of the variables significantly differentiated successful and unsuccessful Arts and Science men, two revealed differences for Engineering men, six for Arts and Science women, and 12 for women in Education. In general, however, it appeared that traits and characteristics related to high achievement vary both between the sexes and the different colleges. High achieving females in Education seem to share characteristics with low achieving males in Arts and Science, for example.

Rosenkrantz, Paul; Bee, Helen; Vogel, Susan; Broverman, Inge; and Broverman, Donald M. "Sex-Role Stereotypes and Self-Concepts in College Students." *Journal of Consulting and Clinical Psychology*, 1968 (Jun),32(3),287-295.

A study of the relationship of self-concept to differences in valued sex-role stereotypes that found strong agreement between sexes about differences between men and women; agreement between men and women that a greater number of the characteristics and behaviors stereotyped as masculine are socially desirable than those stereotyped as feminine; and an agreement between the self-concept of men and women and stereotypes for the two sexes. The last finding suggests, in the authors' opinion, that women hold negative values of their worth relative to men.

Seashore, Harold. "Women Are More Predictable Than Men." *Journal of Counseling Psychology*, 1962(Fall),9(3),261-270.

Report of study indicating that women's grade-point averages are more apt to correlate more highly with scores on tests of academic ability than are men's, on the average.

Sewell, William H., and Shaw, Vimal P. "Socio-economic Status, Intelligence and the Attainment of Higher Education." *Sociology of Education*, 1967(Winter),40(1),1-23.

Drawing on data from questionnaires administered to all Wisconsin high school seniors in 1957, and on follow-up questionnaires returned by approximately one-third (9,007) of the original group, this study reports effects of socioeconomic and intelligence factors on college plans, college attendance, and college graduation; variables include SES, intelligence, college plans, attendance and graduation, and educational attainment. Although the converse was found to be the case for men, for all women, socioeconomic status continued to be a more significant factor than intelligence in collegiate aspirations. For college students, intelligence tended to be more significant in determining who graduated than did SES which, however, still exerted some influence. College plans of girls tended to be more realistic than boys' plans. Combined effects of intelligence and SES on all phases of college aspirations for both sexes were generally "positive, monotonic, and statistically significant."

Stricker, George. "Intellective and Non-intellective Correlates of Grade Point Average." *American Psychologist,* 1964(Jul),20(7),487.
The GPA's of more than 400 students were correlated with scores on 3 intellective and 10 nonintellective variables. The only nonintellective variables to relate to GPA were sex and major area of study.

Thompson, O. E. "Occupational Values of High School Students." *Personnel and Guidance Journal,* 1966(Apr),44(8),850-853.
In this study, it was found that although occupational values differ practically not at all between the freshman and sophomore years, females tend to place less importance than men on leadership jobs, high-paying or recognition-achievement jobs; they place more emphasis than men on self-expression and other-oriented jobs. No sex differentiation appeared on the following variables: interesting, security, independence.

Tomeh, Aida K. "The Impact of Reference Groups on the Educational and Occupational Aspirations of Women College Students." *Journal of Marriage and the Family,* 1968(Feb),30(1),102-110.
434, of 523, 18-23-year-old women enrolled as full-time students at Beirut College for Women responded to a questionnaire on the importance of reference groups on their educational and occupational aspirations. As a total group, or as defined by SES, religion, size of hometown, and nationality, these women indicated that parents had significant impact on college plans (the higher the SES, the greater the father's influence and the greater his influence over the mother; in low SES other family members tended to have some impact; mother's and father's were of equal influence), that brothers and sisters had some impact, that teachers, counselors, and other adults had practically none. Self-assertion was maintained in specifics of the college decision but had equal impact to parents' in graduate plans. Sample not representative but articulate. Commentary on significance of nuclear family in contemporary Mid-East culture.

Torcivia, James M., and Laughlin, Patrick R. "Dogmatism and Concept-Attainment Strategies." *Journal of Personality and Social Psychology,* 1968(Apr),8(4),397-400.
A study of high dogmatic and low dogmatic female high school students (as differentiated by the Rokeach Dogmatism Scale) resulted in findings that indicate high dogmatic females are less able to organize new beliefs and integrate them into their already existing belief system in problem solving.

Tulkin, Steven R. "Race, Class, Family, and School Achievement." *Journal of Personality and Social Psychology,* 1968(May),9(1),31-37.
Among other findings, a multivariate analysis of variance on intelligence and

achievement tests with and without covariate controls has shown that the sex effect is highly significant in lower and upper SES groups. The data were also examined to determine if certain racial differences discussed are found in both females and males. Reanalysis of the racial differences controlling for sex showed that in the upper SES group all of the significant differences were attributable to racial differences between the male groups, while none of the differences between female groups reached an acceptable level of significance. At the lower SES level, for the most part, the pattern was reversed and differences were more significant in the female group. Some sex differences in correlations were also obtained when the data concerning correlations between total achievement and other major variables were analyzed separately by sex groups.

Tyler, Leona E. "Differences between Men and Women," in Tyler, Leona E., *The Psychology of Human Differences.* New York: Appleton-Century, 1947. Chapter 4.
Sex differences revealed by psychological tests and other measures available during the first half of the century in areas such as: school achievement, intellect, tested abilities, interests, attitudes, personal characteristics.

Werts, C. E. "Sex Differences in College Attendance." *National Merit Scholarship Corporation Research Reports*, 1966,2,1-11.
Socioeconomic factors are more apt to deter girls than boys from college attendance, academic ability being equal. Girls from low-status homes were significantly less likely to go on to college than boys of similar backgrounds.

Wineman, John H. "Sex Differences on the Hidden Figures Test." *Experimental Publication System*, 1971(Apr),11,Ms. No. 416-24.
Using the Hidden Figures Test to assess sex differences in field-independence in perception, French, Ekstrom, and Price found no significant differences between the sexes on this trait; in fact, the mean score for women was slightly higher than the mean for men. The study is of interest since its findings are contrary to those of Witkin (listed herein), who used the Rod-and-Frame Test and the Embedded Figures Test in his study. Wineman speculates that the French, and others, sample may have been skewed in the direction of individuals with nurturing interests and/or that the Hidden Figures Test measures a similar but not identical factor.

Witkin, Herman A.; Kyk, Ruth B.; Faterson, Hannah F.; Goodenough, Donald R.; and Karp, Stephen A. *Psychological Differentiation.* New York and London: John Wiley & Sons, 1962.
This work analyzes interrelationships of cognitive and personality aspects of psychological development and stability of these patterns from early family experience through their development in social functioning. Chapter 13 (pp. 214-221) deals specifically with sex differences in modes of perception and

their sources and intellectual functioning as well as the effect of a mother's character and her interaction with her child(ren).

Wyer, Robert S., and Terrell, Glenn. "Social Role and Academic Achievement." *Journal of Personality and Social Psychology,* **1965(Jul),2(1), 117-121.**
For this study, 28 males and 28 females, drawn from a larger sample of primarily sophomores from various University of Colorado colleges, were divided by sex into four groups according to achievement and performance levels in order to investigate the relationship of social role to academic achievement. Analyses were made by groups of: (1) desire to receive social and academic recognition; (2) certainty of occupational choice; (3) self-sufficiency; and (4) self-control or persistence. Findings indicate that high achievement-low potential females and low achievement-high potential females were more certain of occupational choice than the two other female groups whose achievement and performance were compatible; a controlled, exacting will-power related negatively to academic performance among females (converse appeared true for males); and males more than females seem to feel a conflict between social and academic goals.

4. Educational Behavior and Aspirations of High School Students

Anderson, Dale G., and Heimann, Robert A. "Vocational Maturity of Junior High Girls." *Vocational Guidance Quarterly*, 1967(Mar),15(3), 191-195.
Research findings indicate that a short-term exposure to vocational counseling effectively increased vocational maturation of eighth-grade girls.

Astin, Helen S. "Career Development of Girls during the High School Years." *Journal of Counseling Psychology*, 1968(Nov),15(6),536-540.
Correlation of observable personal and social characteristics of 817 ninth-grade girls with the types of career choices made by them in the twelfth grade, allowing for variable factors such as school size and early vocational counseling; larger schools seem to provide more career stimulus for girls; girls who in the twelfth grade anticipated teaching or science careers tended to report college counseling experience in the ninth grade; girls who reported having had job counseling in the ninth grade were more apt to select office work and housewife occupations more frequently than those having had no job counseling.

Astin, Helen S. "Stability and Change in the Career Plans of Ninth-Grade Girls." *Personnel and Guidance Journal*, 1968(Jun),46(10),961-966.
Longitudinal study of 11,809 girls, their career choices as ninth-graders in 1960 and as high school graduates in 1964, and their aptitude and interest scores. Occupations involved were classified as "career" or "noncareer." Study findings support the hypothesis that brighter girls tended to stay in the "career" occupations or defect to "career" from "noncareer" fields over the course of the high school years and that less scholastically capable girls tend to remain in the "noncareer" fields or defect to them from the "career" occupations.

Cross, Patricia K. *New Students to Higher Education.* San Francisco: Jossey-Bass, in preparation.
"The largest reservoir of academically well-qualified young people who are not now attending college are women from the lower socioeconomic levels."

Dauw, Dean C. "Career Choices of High and Low Creative Thinkers." *Vocational Guidance Quarterly*, 1966(Dec),15(2),135-140.
Dauw notes an association of creative thinking level and occupational choice among boys and girls in the twelfth grade. Some findings include: a greater proportion of highly creative girls were classified as seeking for careers in General Culture or Arts and Entertainment than in Service, Organization, Technology, Science, or Outdoor career categories; girls with low creative

ability selected Organization in significantly large numbers. 253 of the 351 boys in the study listed 76 occupations not listed by any girl; 227 of the 361 girls listed 35 occupations not listed by a single boy; there were 41 occupations listed by at least one boy and one girl.

Douvan, Elizabeth, and Adelson, Joseph. *The Adolescent Experience.* **New York: John Wiley & Sons, Inc., 1966.**
Includes comprehensive coverage of sex differences in a variety of adolescent behaviors and patterns of development.

Droege, Robert C. "Sex Differences in Aptitude Maturation during High School." *Journal of Counseling Psychology*, 1967(Sep),14(5),407-411.
A longitudinal investigation of the effects of maturation on aptitude scores. A general population sample of high school students were given the GATB in grades 9, 10, and 11 and retested with an alternate form in grade 12. Another sample was tested in grade 12 only. Findings indicated that for both sexes the average increases in aptitude scores attributable to practice and maturation were about the same, as was the correlation between the initial and retest scores. Girls maintained higher mean scores in Form Perception, Clerical Perception, Motor Coordination, and Finger Dexterity; there appeared a greater tendency for score stability for girls in Motor Coordination than for boys.

Flanagan, John, and associates. *The American High School Student.* **Pittsburgh, Pa.: Project TALENT Office, University of Pittsburgh, 1964.**
In this study of academic motivation, girls display a greater tendency toward consistent scholastic effort than do boys.

Fortner, Mildred L. "Vocational Choices of High School Girls: Can They Be Predicted?" *Vocational Guidance Quarterly*, 1970(Mar),18(3),203-206.
Report of a study of 400 junior and senior high school girls to determine predictability of vocational choices; intelligence alone proved to be as strong an index as when compounded with self-concept and parental occupational level.

Harkness, Charles A. "The Vocational Aspirations of the Disadvantaged Girl." *Journal of Employment Counseling*, 1970(Mar),7(1),19-25.
Study of aspirations of 415 16- to 21-year-old girls of all racial groups entering Urban Job Corps programs reveals a history of being discouraged from entering skilled trades and a dearth of professional counseling material for the noncollege oriented individual.

Hathaway, Starke R.; Reynolds, Phyllis C.; and Monachesi, Elio D. "Follow-up of 812 Girls in 10 Years after High School Dropout." *Journal of Consulting and Clinical Psychology*, 1969(Aug),33(4),383-390.
This study compared a dropout and a nondropout group on several variables with data pre- and post-dating time of dropout. The groups were subdivided

by time of marriage and intelligence. Findings indicate that dropouts have a higher separation and divorce rate, even when the time of marriage is controlled, that they have larger families but apparently only because of the longer length of marriage, and that they are from lower socioeconomic statuses generally; only girls from blue-collar families show downward social mobility. When grouped by intelligence, high and middle intelligence in dropouts does not correlate positively with upward mobility as is the case with nondropouts.

King, Karl; McIntyre, Jennie; and Axelson, Leland J. "Adolescents' Views of Maternal Employment as a Threat to the Marital Relationship." *Journal of Marriage and the Family,* 1968(Nov),30(4),633-637.
Results of this study of ninth graders' perceptions indicate that maternal employment is viewed as less of a threat to the husband-wife relationship by adolescents with working mothers and by adolescents of a higher socioeconomic background. Male adolescents perceived the effect of maternal employment upon this relationship to be greater than did female adolescents. Adolescents of both sexes (although females slightly more) were inclined to accept maternal employment in positive proportion to the father's participation in household tasks.

Knoell, Dorothy M. *People Who Need College: A Report on Students We Have Yet to Serve.* Washington, D.C.: American Association of Junior Colleges, 1970.
Documents the effect of low family income and minority group status on college attendance for girls.

Moerk, Ernst, and Becker, Penelope. "Attitudes of High School Students Toward Future Marriage and College Education." *The Family Coordinator,* 1971(Jan),20(1),67-73.
Study of attitudes of 168 female and 119 male students in a high school located in a lower-class neighborhood; the students were between the ages of 14 and 17. Although the total number of girls pursuing education is increasing, the older girls in this sample, findings indicate, perceive college as less significant a factor in their futures than do younger girls and all boys.

Nelson, Helen Y., and Goodman, Phyllis R. "Attitudes of High School Students and Young Adults toward the Gainful Employment of Married Women." *The Family Coordinator,* 1969(Jul),18(3),251-255.
Concise report of attitudes of high school students questioned in 1959 and again in 1966 and of high school students queried in 1965; findings reveal an increase in acceptance of the concept of a wife's employment although almost all the males, projecting 5 to 10 years into the future, indicated a desire for a wife who was a homemaker only.

Progress toward the Goals of Project TALENT Bulletin No. 4. Pittsburgh, Pa.: Project TALENT Office, University of Pittsburgh, February 1965.

Assessment of progress toward stated goals. Emphasis on career selection in relation to aptitude and ability (for girls, only teacher, nurse, and secretary are dealt with at length) and career pattern stability; and on differences in high school ability and achievement patterns. In regard to the latter emphasis, girls seem to lose more scientific knowledge than they retain over the period from grade 9 to 12; to increase mathematical knowledge only between the ninth and tenth grades and then cease to show perceptible gains; and to show a steady increase in mean scores over the four years in certain language skills (not including Vocabulary or Reading Comprehension) alone.

Project TALENT *One-Year Follow-up Studies.* Pittsburgh, Pa.: Project TALENT Office, University of Pittsburgh, 1966.
Review of findings, based on data from follow-up surveys one year after high school graduation and interpreted by sex, SES, and scores on aptitude and knowledge measures, regarding: educational aspirations, probabilities of attendance, and actual attendance at college; major fields of study; jobs held after high school; career aspirations and stability patterns. (For girls, teacher and housewife were the only occupations showing more than 50 percent stability from any grade level to one year after high school.)

Rezler, Agnes G. "Characteristics of High School Girls Choosing Traditional or Pioneer Vocations." *Personnel and Guidance Journal*, 1967 (Mar),45(7),659-665.
By their junior year in high school, this study indicates, pioneers can be identified through their efforts to fight their own fears as well as culture, and by their need to integrate self-concepts with reality.

Schab, Fred. "Marriage and the High School Student." *Journal of the National Association of Women Deans and Counselors*, 1970(Fall), 34(1),34-37.
Views on various marriage conditions held by students in 11 high schools in northeastern Georgia were analyzed by sex, age, academic ability, and race. Trends indicated by the findings include: white girls were more interested in marriage during high school than other groups (no Negro girl indicated this interest); academically talented males comprised the largest group wishing to postpone marriage until after college, academically poor males until after they secured a good job, females until the right person came along; males were the most unconcerned group regarding religious differences, whites regarding parental desires, and white females were the most concerned regarding heredity. Unrepresentative sample reflects cultural, socioeconomic, and racial restrictions.

Shaycroft, Marion F. *The High School Years: Growth in Cognitive Skills.* Pittsburgh, Pa.: Project TALENT Office, 1967.
In this study investigating the changes in students' abilities during the high school years and factors that produced them, the two sexes showed different

patterns of mental growth between grades 9 and 12. Boys seemed to acquire significantly more information than girls in many areas and also had larger score gains on several aptitude tests. Tests on which girls made significantly greater gains than boys included Literature Information, Memory for Words, Spelling, and Home Economics Information. The sex showing the larger average gain on the tests (except Literature Information) was also the one with the higher mean score in grade 9.

Sterrett, Joyce E., and Bollman, Stephen R. "Factors Related to Adolescents' Expectation of Marital Roles." *The Family Coordinator*, 1970 (Oct),19(4),353-356.
Study of 100 girls and boys which found that marriage role expectations were more equalitarian among younger students, those of higher social status, and those with higher grade point averages but these expectations were not affected by the employment status of the mother. Male expectations in the area of homemaking were more equalitarian than the girls'; girls' expectations were more equalitarian in the areas of personal characteristics, financial support, and employment.

Torrance, E. Paul. "Helping the Creatively Gifted Girl Achieve Her Potentiality." *Journal of the National Association of Women Deans and Counselors*, 1965(Fall),29(1),28-33.
Using constructive, nonhabitual response to change and stress as an index of creative potential, the author suggests six roles for counselors to adopt for effective guidance and development of this potentiality.

Trent, James W., and Medsker, Leland L. *Beyond High School.* San Francisco: Jossey-Bass, 1968.
Study of 10,000 boys and girls from a variety of regions and schools and tested with the Omnibus Personality Inventory at high school graduation and four years later. College attendance was correlated with "improved" scores on most scales of the inventory. Noteworthy was a marked decline in measures of intellectual disposition among girls who became full-time homemakers.

Winkler, Mary Carlyle. "High School Ability Patterns: A Backward Look from the Doctorate." *Journal of the National Association of Women Deans and Counselors*, 1966(Summer),29(4),177-179.
High school records of doctorate holders were reviewed in 1958 and in 1962 and compared with the records of classmates who had not earned the doctorate. Despite the numerical increase in doctorate holders over the four years, there was found to be no measurable difference in high school patterns over that period. Doctorate holders on the average remained 1.5 standard deviations above the mean of the general population in measured ability. Although in a random sample of classmates boys excelled on intelligence and standardized tests, girls made better grades. Women who were married at the time of receipt of the doctorate were more apt to be superior high school stu-

dents than were their unmarried colleagues. Conversely, men who were bachelors upon receipt of the doctorate were more apt to be superior students in high school than were married male recipients. The highest high school records for doctorate holders were found in the Northeast, in independent schools, and in the cases of those who had earned doctorates in the "hard sciences."

5. Educational Behavior and Aspirations of College Students

Almquist, Elizabeth M., and Angrist, Shirley S. "Career Salience and Atypicality of Occupational Choice among College Women." *Journal of Marriage and the Family*, 1970(May),32(2),242-249.
With the focus on college women choosing male-typed occupations this study disproves the hypothesis that such women are "deviants" and suggests that the basis for atypical career choice is rather the effect of more broadening and enriching experience. Sample is small (110) and the research instruments consisted of 4 questionnaires and 2 interviews over a four-year period.

American Council on Education. *National Norms for Entering College Freshmen–Fall, 1970.* ACE Research Report No. 6. Washington, D.C.: Office of Research, American Council on Education, 1970.
Includes data on sex differences in college enrollment, characteristics of freshmen, and selected expectations and attitudes.

Astin, Alexander W., and Panos, Robert J. *The Educational and Vocational Development of College Students.* Washington, D.C.: American Council on Education, 1969.
Third in a series of studies originally dealing with 127,000 students (for this study, 36,000) entering colleges and universities as freshmen in 1961. Report assesses significance of institutional type on undergraduates' educational aspirations and career plans. Extensive data describe the class of 1965, personal and environmental factors that affect students' achievement as well as choice of major field of study and career planning during the undergraduate years. Findings are summarized by institutional type and, as a control, by sex, race, and geographic region. Women's colleges show no significant influence on undergraduate aspirations except for a slight tendency to direct students' interests from teaching to the social sciences. Men's colleges and women's colleges also seem to develop in their students graduate school aspirations to a greater extent than do coeducational institutions. It was also discovered that the dropout rate for both men and women is greater if a coeducational institution is attended, and this appears true even for high ability women students.

Baine, Emmie V. "Women Holders of Leadership Positions on the Coeducational Campus." *Journal of the National Association of Women Deans and Counselors*, 1968(Fall),32(1),39-40.
187 of 265 colleges and universities replied to a questionnaire concerning women in leadership positions; responses indicated that in all-student organizations there were 8 female presidents, 44 female vice presidents, 147 female secretaries, and 26 female treasurers. Other responses concerning women's

organizations and their autonomy lead author to highlight the need for more autonomous women's associations as part of the development of collegiate programs directed toward special needs of women.

Conaway, Christine Y., and Niple, Mary Lou. "The Working Patterns of Mothers and Grandmothers of Freshman Women at the Ohio State University, 1955 and 1965." *Journal of the National Association of Women Deans and Counselors*, 1966(Summer),29(4),167-170.
Comparison of studies done 10 years apart on family employment statistics, student goals and aspirations; data indicate a significant increase in the employment of mothers and a concomitant increase in career commitment among the third generation.

Cook, Barbara. "Roles, Labels, Stereotypes: A Counselor's Challenge." *Journal of the National Association of Women Deans and Counselors*, 1971(Spring),34(3),99-105.
Contains specific recommendations for counselor action to help young women prepare for full participation in their society, including the need to understand the realities of that society, recognition of personal prejudices about women's status, active opposition to sex discrimination in the counselor's institution, provision of non-sex-typed role models for both sexes, administration of the Male and Female SVIB to both men and women students, examination of presentation of sex-role stereotypes in institutional literature, and aggression in defending and expanding the counselor's own status as a woman and as a professional.

Cox, Mary B., and Van Dusen, William D. "How Educational Borrowing Affects the Female Student." *College Board Review*, 1969(Spring),71, 28-31.
Report of a 55 percent return from a survey of alumnae of 1962 and 1964 graduating classes of selective Eastern women's colleges who had borrowed more than $250 during undergraduate years. Borrowing appeared to have no effects on marital status, childbearing, or on graduate education (some evidence that borrowing may encourage entering and persisting in the last). Although 64 percent of the 1962 borrowers and 44 percent of the 1964 borrowers had repaid their loans in full, there was evidence that the borrowers were more apt than nonborrowers to borrow for other purposes. Borrowing did not appear to affect choice of career.

Cross, K. Patricia. "College Women: A Research Description." *Journal of the National Association of Women Deans and Counselors*, 1968(Fall), 32(1),12-21.
Review of American Council on Education research findings of a study of development during college years through direct observation and self-reports. Author is led to conclude that differences in expectations of life fulfillment imply different emphases on life purposes for the two sexes.

Cross, K. Patricia. *The Undergraduate Woman.* Research Report No. 5. Washington, D.C.: American Association for Higher Education, 1971.
Synthesis of research on the undergraduate woman presented to prompt educators' assessment of course of action appropriate to and concomitant with the feminist movement. Major points reported include: estimate that by 1978 45 percent of the national college student population will be women (in 1948, it was 30 percent); estimate that the typical high school female graduate will spend 25 years in the labor force; sex differentials on measures of ability have been consistent, with women scoring higher than men in areas such as English, Humanities; women gain consistently higher grades from elementary school through high school and college and show greater motivation to achieve academic success than do men.

Darling, Ruth W. "College Women: Do They Fit the Research Description?" *Journal of the National Association of Women Deans and Counselors,* 1968(Fall),32(1),22-25.
Author supports Cross' description *(College Women: A Research Description)* but argues that perceptions of relevance in education are not necessarily a function of sex differences alone and that both men and women need greater flexibility in educative processes.

Davis, James A. *Great Aspirations: The Graduate School Plans of America's College Seniors.* National Opinion Research Center: Monographs in Social Research. Chicago: Aldine Publishing Company, 1964.
Based on a large sample of classes graduating from American colleges and universities in 1961, this study investigates their graduate school plans in relation to variables such as SES, race, sex, religion, and demographic characteristics. While 60 percent of the sample were men, the women in general were characterized by high SES, superior academic performance, and had social rather than economic interests invested in postgraduate plans. A small proportion of the women intended to be housewives exclusively; of those who did 1 percent still had graduate school aspirations. Motivational, rationale, and economic factors associated with graduate school plans are discussed as well as future fields of graduate study, delineated by sex.

Davis, James A. *Undergraduate Career Decisions: Correlates of Occupational Choice.* National Opinion Research Center: Monographs in Social Research. Chicago: Aldine Publishing Company, 1965.
Originally part of Davis' study noted above, these findings deal with ambivalence and stability in career planning of undergraduates. Analysis of relationship of sex, academic performance, values, and background of students who plan to enter the fields of: education, social sciences, law, biological sciences, business, humanities and fine arts, engineering, medicine, and the physical sciences.

Elton, Charles F., and Rose, Harriett A. "Significance of Personality in the Vocational Choice of College Women." *Journal of Counseling Psychology*, 1967(Jul),14(4),293-298.

To study significance of personality and aptitude predictors in vocational choice among freshmen women, this report assesses the influence of five personality scores and one scholastic aptitude score on the vocational choice of all the female freshmen entering a particular university in 1965. The scores were on the OPI factors: Tolerance and Autonomy, Suppression-Repression, Masculine Role, Scholarly Orientation, and Social Introversion. The ACT score was used for scholastic aptitude measure. Analysis of these scores and vocational choice indicates both intellectual and personality differences among the various occupational choices. Implications for counseling, the authors conclude, are clear inasmuch as, in their opinion, vocational choice can be linked to personality traits.

Eyde, Lorraine D. *Work Values and Background Factors as Predictors of Women's Desire to Work*. Columbus, Ohio: Ohio State University, Bureau of Business Research Monograph No. 108, 1962.

Motivations for work among women are explored in 130 cases of women college seniors and alumnae with reference to such factors as: marital status; financial status; number and age of children; activity involvement in college; socioeconomic status; occupation and education of parents; and values.

Faunce, Patricia Spencer. "Academic Careers of Gifted Women." *Personnel and Guidance Journal*, 1967(Nov),46(3),252-257.

Part of an earlier study, this report analyzes the careers of gifted women (graduates and nongraduates) in relation to length of academic attendance, major fields of study, degrees and honors conferred, and counseling bureau contact. Graduates differed significantly from nongraduates in GPA, amount of contact with the counseling bureau (43.6 percent to 30.9 percent), and major fields of study (for graduates, the major fields included social science, interdepartmental or double, education, and home economics; for nongraduates, English, linguistics and languages, natural sciences and mathematics, and business administration).

Faunce, Patricia Spencer. "Personality Characteristics and Vocational Interests Related to the College Persistence of Academically Gifted Women." *Journal of Counseling Psychology*, 1968(Jan),15(1),31-40.

To explore the influence of nonintellective variables on the persistence of academically gifted women in college and to see if these nonintellective variables could be identified at the beginning of the freshman year, 249 academically gifted female freshmen, entering a liberal arts college during the fall quarters of 1950 through 1958 were administered the MMPI and the SVIB. Transcripts of these students were examined in 1964 to identify graduate and nongraduate status. MMPI scores showed graduate students (723) to have been, in their freshman year, more insightful, conventional, temperate, modest, self-confident, relatively free from tension, and more secure in ego-strength and psychological integration; nongraduates (526) had less insight into their own personality structures, greater difficulty in inter-personal relationships, more problems with impulse control and greater inner tensions. SVIB scores of graduates were higher on the author, librarian, English teacher, social science teacher, psychologist, and lawyer scales. Nongraduates scored highly on the buyer, stenography-secretary, office worker, business education teacher, and dietician scales. Personal characteristics and vocational interests determined in the freshman year appear to influence scholastic persistence.

Faunce, Patricia S. "Withdrawal of Academically Gifted Women." *Journal of The National Association of Women Deans and Counselors*, 1968 (May),9(3),171-176.

According to frequency and percentage, those leading reasons of 23 (marriage, insufficient finances, no major or dissatisfaction with major, work or good job opportunity, personal problems or immaturity), given by academically gifted women who withdrew from college, suggest to the author that these women would have welcomed and benefited from counseling assistance. Follow-up letters from the withdrawals confirm this. Random sample of 526 women was taken from withdrawals from the University of Minnesota.

Gottsdanker, Josephine S. "Intellectual Interest Patterns of Gifted College Students." *Educational and Psychological Measurement*, 1968 (Summer),28(2), 361-366.

75 gifted male college students and 75 gifted female college students were studied in comparison with 75 males and 75 females selected at random regarding their intellectual interests. The gifted students, in general, showed significantly higher scores on scales indicating intellectual commitments, interest in abstractions, and desire for independent thought. When the sexes were compared, however, the gifted women showed significant differences and differed most greatly from the typical women in their interest in theoretical problems, desires for independence, and attraction to self-initiated intellectual endeavors. Gifted men showed less social introversion than the unselected men but the gifted women were not different from the unselected females on the scale. According to measures derived from the OPI, gifted women show a different pattern of intellectual interests than do the men and they are far more divergent from average students than are the gifted men. They are outstandingly interested in independent thought.

Gysbers, Norman C.; Johnston, Joseph A.; and Gust, Tim. "Characteristics of Homemaker- and Career-Oriented Women." *Journal of Counseling Psychology*, 1968(Nov),15(6),541-546.

Report of a longitudinal study of college women classified by their Strong Vocational Interest Blank for Women profiles as either homemaker or career-oriented. There was some support for the predictive validity of the scale but also evidence that social class, education, parents' education, other family background variables, and personality characteristics not measured by the SVIB, plus differences in the importance attached to work may be more predictive than the shape of the interest profile.

Harmon, Lenore W. "The Predictive Power over Ten Years of Measured Social Service and Scientific Interests among College Women." *Journal of Applied Psychology*, 1969(Jun),53(3,Pt.1),193-196.

A little more than one-third of the women who had high scores on the SVIB-W Social Workers and Laboratory Technician scales in 1953-55 had kept career commitment 10 years later. Equal in validity to men's scores and commitment, but not an index that can, in the author's opinion, be used to identify persons whose career commitment will be high.

Katz, Joseph. "Career and Autonomy in College Women," in Katz, Joseph, and others, *Class, Character, and Career*. Stanford, Calif.: Institute for the Study of Human Problems, Stanford University, 1968.

The CPI, the SVIB, and a 115-item questionnaire relating to occupational choice and work values were administered to a random sample of students at a four-year residential college (686) and at a two-year non-residential college (448). Response findings indicated that women planning to be housewives, as compared to women planning careers, tended to be more security minded and to want more economic affluence. Among women planning careers, only those planning to go into business had income expectations as high as did the prospective housewives. While the group of women planning to be housewives was large and varied, more women among them tended to have a passive orientation toward life. However, the women at the relatively affluent four-year college who were planning to be housewives reported higher self-esteem than their classmates, while the reverse was true at the less affluent two-year college. The following factors were found to influence career choice and contribute to inappropriate career choices: (1) incomplete identity information; (2) social class; (3) culture or mores; (4) parental expectations and the student's perception of these expectations; (5) student's identification with parents; (6) significant peers, especially boy friends or fiancés; (7) the college experience (a) directly through occupational experiences and (b) indirectly through experiences that helped to develop and stabilize the self-concept; (8) occupational opportunities, or the student's perception of what occupations are available.

Katz, Joseph, and associates. *No Time for Youth*. San Francisco: Jossey-Bass, 1968.

Based on interviews and an extensive collection of data derived from instruments administered to 3,500 entering Berkeley and Stanford freshmen in 1961 and continued over a four-year period, this book investigates the undergraduate student in regard to his personality developmental processes and how they are affected by growth and conditions of constraint during the four college years; the different ways in which students learn, and the different types of students and the lives they live on and off campus. Both survey data and interview materials reveal a number of sex differences in aspects of personal development during the college years, including family relationships, peer group associations, sexuality, career plans, and in response to academic and social factors in the college environment.

Kirkbridge, Virginia R. "Project Lifeline Introduces College Women to Their Futures." *Journal of the National Association of Women Deans and Counselors*, 1966(Summer),29(4),174-176.
Description of a program led by upperclassmen to enable freshmen to consider the scope and quality of current education and its implications for future career and life-span.

Leland, Carole A., and Lozoff, Marjorie M. *College Influences on the Role Development of Female Undergraduates*. Stanford, Calif.: Institute for the Study of Human Problems, Stanford University, 1966.
In Part I, a bibliographical essay, Leland presents a critique of the research literature of the 1950s and 1960s, defining its shortcomings and narrow perspectives. Lozoff, in Part II, reports her analysis of interview data from 49 college women and describes differences in parental influence, self-evaluations, and behaviors as these shaped career development and perception of the female role.

Lloyd, Betty-Jane. "A Questionnaire Portrait of the Freshman Coed: After College, What?" *Journal of the National Association of Women Deans and Counselors*, 1966(Summer),29(4),159-162.
Although the study reported reveals a rise in percentage of those considering graduate school and an increase of intended years in the labor force after only one semester of college work, no research on the stability of these attitudes and aspirations is presented — leaving malleability of this age group the only valid inference.

Lloyd, Betty-Jane. "Retouched Picture: Follow-Up of a Questionnaire Portrait of the Freshman Coed." *Journal of the National Association of Women Deans and Counselors*, 1967(Summer),30(4),174-177.
In this study initiated in 1963, 95 students at a women's college on a coed campus responded at the beginning and end of their first semester to questionnaires concerning their views on early adjustment to college and to their lives beyond college. Follow-up questionnaires were received by 59 of the original sample at the end of their junior year. Response comparison (of such items as choice of college, major field, satisfactions, future goals, marriage-work roles) indicated, for the most part, general group retention of earlier views, although individual responses varied significantly. Ideas and attitudes of young women do not appear to change drastically within a period of a few college years but seem to come into clearer focus for the individual student.

McKeachie, Wilbert J., and Lin, Yi-Guang. "Sex Differences in Student Response to College Teachers: Teacher Warmth and Teacher Sex." *American Educational Research Journal*, 1971(Mar),8(2),221-226.

This study reports that women teachers, with a warm, interpersonally oriented teaching style, have a positive effect on the academic achievement of both male and female students; male teachers, with the same teaching style, have a positive effect on the academic achievement of females and on the academic achievement of males high in Need Affiliation.

McMillin, Marvin R.; Cerra, Patrick F.; and Mehaffey, Thomas D. "Opinions on Career Involvement of Married Women." *Journal of the National Association of Women Deans and Counselors*, 1971(Spring),34(3), 121-124.

Subjects of the study were 1,817 women (a 60.6 percent response) and 1,085 men (a 42.3 percent response) college students in a moderate sized midwestern university. Almost 72 percent of the women indicated a preference for working after marriage until children were born, then devoting full time to the family while the children were young and returning to work when children are older; 8 percent preferred to work in a profession continuously after marriage. 40 percent of the men stated a preference for their wives to return to work when the children were older; 38 percent preferred that their wives not work after marriage unless absolutely necessary; and 12 percent preferred that their wives not work at all after marriage. Both men and women were less apt to take the option of "no further career after marriage" in the senior year than in the freshman year. For women, the option decreased from almost 4 percent in the freshman year to less than 1 percent in the senior year; for men, from almost 14 percent to less than 2 percent. 39 percent of freshman men preferred that the wife reenter her profession when the children were older, but 52 percent of senior men so preferred.

Mitterling, Philip I., ed. *Needed Research on Able Women in Honors Programs, College and Society*. Proceedings of the Conference on Talented Women and the American College. Sponsored by the Inter-university Committee on the Superior Student and the United States Office of Education, in cooperation with the School of General Studies, Columbia University. Cooperative Research Project No. F-028. Washington, D.C.: U. S. Department of Health, Education, and Welfare, 1964.

Proceedings of a conference of 75 participants designed to identify educational and societal problems for the undergraduate woman, to instigate new concepts of solving these problems, and to determine the approaches and requirements for future research on the topic. Includes addresses by Diana Trilling ("The Influence of Contemporary Literary Culture on the Gifted College Woman"); David Riesman ("Women in Higher Education: Problems and Prospects"); Bruno Bettelheim ("The Talented Woman in American Society"); and Paul A. Heist ("Research on Talented Women: Problems of Appropriate and Adequate Sources of Data").

Morrill, Weston H.; Miller, C. Dean; and Thomas, Lucinda E. "Educational and Vocational Interests of College Women." *Vocational Guidance Quarterly,* 1970(Dec),19(2),85-89.

The SVIB-W and the Educational Interest Inventory were administered to 109 female students who requested counseling at a university counseling center over a period of three years. Correlation of scores on the two instruments indicate a high proportion of variance not common to both interest scales; one set of interests cannot safely be predicted from the other.

Murphy, Lois B., and Raushenbush, Esther, eds. *Achievement in the College Years: A Record of Intellectual and Personal Growth.* New York: Harpers, 1960.

Report of a study, conducted by the Sarah Lawrence faculty, of a group of college students during their four years of college and for two years beyond to assess the trends in students' personality dynamics, intellectual achievement, vocational orientation, and development of intellectual qualities through the four years of college experience.

Norfleet, Mary Ann Warburton. "Personality Characteristics of Achieving and Underachieving High Ability Senior Women." *Personnel and Guidance Journal,* 1968(Jun),46(10),976-980.

A carefully selected group of 29 achievers and 26 underachievers was administered the California Personality Inventory and the Gough Adjective Check List in an effort to determine differential characteristics in these senior class, university women. Achievers distinguished themselves from nonachievers on eight scales of the CPI which suggest that the achievers are more poised, responsible, mature, and tolerant. The two groups described themselves differently on the Check List: achievers describe themselves as capable, conscientious, and industrious; underachievers thought of themselves as civilized, friendly, sentimental, sociable, thoughtful, and understanding. The author suggests the findings indicate that the underachiever is less adequately socialized than the achiever.

Roe, Anne, and Siegleman, Marvin. *The Origin of Interests.* American Personnel and Guidance Inquiry Studies, No. 1, 1964.

A study of college seniors and of men and women engineers and men and women social workers supported the hypothesis that choice of occupation is affected by childhood experiences. It appeared that "the farther from the cultural sex stereotype the occupational choice is, the more likely it is that there have been particular pressures in the early histories that influenced such a choice." The male social workers and the female engineers had more specific and extensive early background pressures than the female social workers and the male engineers. Thus, it appeared that the occupation itself seemed to offer a replacement for earlier wants: for example, love and understanding in the case of men social workers, a lost father in the case of women engineers.

Schmidt, Marlin R. "Personality Change in College Women." *Journal of College Student Personnel*, 1970(Nov),11(6),414-418.

314 women participated in this investigation of personality changes over the four-year college period. Compared to themselves as freshmen, seniors had more positive self-regard, were more apt to prefer "female" occupations, exhibited no significant change in graduate school aspirations, were less likely to value marriage over vocational training, and felt more interpersonally competent.

Schufletowski, Frank W. "Are College Women Satisfied with Their Equality and Freedom?" *Journal of College Student Personnel*, 1967(Mar),8 (2),109-111.

Findings indicate that subjects (250) were satisfied with present university rules and regulations. Questions posed to them involved dormitory closing hours, "equality of rights" as compared with men's rights, control of own activities, administrative power in affairs of women vs. men, concept of same privileges to freshmen and to seniors, attempts of the university to eliminate double sexual standards, existence of inequality on campus, concern of administration about existent inequality, and acceptance of rules applicable to all students regardless of sex.

Schwartz, Jane. "Medicine as a Vocational Choice among Undergraduate Women." *Journal of the National Association of Women Deans and Counselors*, 1969(Fall),33(1),7-12.

Investigation of characteristics of seniors who, as college freshmen, had indicated an interest in a premedical undergraduate program. No apparent differences were revealed in the background or characteristics of students persisting in premed and of those changing fields. Misconceptions, the author concludes, regarding the medical field appeared to produce the considerable attrition.

Siegel, Alberta E., and Curtis, Elizabeth. "Familial Correlates of Orientation toward Future Employment among College Women." *Journal of Educational Psychology*, 1963(Feb),54(1),33-37.

Of five familial characteristics, only one — mother's work orientation — correlated significantly with the measured work orientation of a random sample of 43 sophomore women at a large university. It is suggested that the sample may have been too homogeneous to sustain any generalizations.

Steinmann, Anne, and Fox, David J. "Attitudes toward Women's Family Role among Black and White Undergraduates." *The Family Coordinator*, 1970(Oct),19(4),363-368.

Report of an investigation which found that black college women perceive man's ideal woman as far less family-oriented and far more self- and action-oriented than any other group of women and that these views were compatible with their opposite sex peers.

Vander Wilt, Robert B., and Klocke, Ronald A. "Self-Actualization of Females in an Experimental Orientation Program." *Journal of the National Association of Women Deans and Counselors*, 1971(Spring),34(3), 125-129.

Subjects of the study were 20 participants (10 male and 10 female) in an Outward Bound Program. Shostrom's Personal Orientation Inventory was used to measure degree of self-actualization (the instrument is based on Maslow's theories). Significant changes were found on nine of the scales on the Shostrom instrument for females and not on four; no significant changes were found among the males as a result of participation in the Outward Bound Program (the experimental orientation program to which the title refers). Thus, while comparison of pre- and post-test scores for the entire group indicated significant changes on 7 of the 12 scales, this result was entirely a function of changes in self-actualization among the female participants.

Vogel, Susan R.; Broverman, Inge K.; Broverman, Donald M.; Clarkson, Frank E.; and Rosenkrantz, Paul S. "Maternal Employment and Perception of Sex Roles among College Students." *Journal of Developmental Psychology*, 1970(Nov),3(3),384-391.

Authors report that mother's employment reduced differential in masculine and feminine role perception for males and, more significantly, for females in comparison with perceptions held by students with homemaker mothers.

Wallace, Walter L. *Student Culture: Social Structure and Continuity in a Liberal Arts College.* National Opinion Research Center, Monographs in Social Research. Chicago: Aldine Publishing Co., 1966. Chapter V, "The Perspective of College Women."

This chapter discusses sex differences within student culture as a whole, and different patterns of sex differences among different student subcultures. Values of large cultures are shown to affect sex differences in values, attitudes, and aspirations. Data from this study conducted at a small midwestern college and specific to the content of this chapter indicate: lower levels of grades orientation and graduate school aspiration among women than among men; the adopted distinction of sex status cut across the more indigenous freshman-nonfreshman distinction; relation of romantic status to grades orientation and graduate school expectation among women was distinctly negative, although freshmen women who enter college already engaged or going steady tended to sustain grades orientation better than the other women; striking contrast in dating satisfactions of sorority and nonsorority women.

Wright, Dorothy M. "Junior College Students View Women's Roles." *Journal of the National Association of Women Deans and Counselors*, 1967 (Winter),30(2),71-77.

Findings of a questionnaire study of junior college students indicate that middle-class student views of women's roles are still, for the most part, traditional.

6. Educational Behavior and Aspirations of Graduate Students

Arregger, Constance E., ed. *Graduate Women at Work.* A Study by a Working Party of the British Federation of University Women. Newcastle upon Tyne, England: Oriel Press, Ltd., 1966.
Comprehensive investigation of the social and domestic patterns of the graduate woman in England and her present situation with regard to future professional employment. Covers the major dimensions of the problem including graduate employment and earnings, marriage, and child-care.

Astin, Helen S. *The Woman Doctorate in America.* New York: Russell Sage Foundation, 1969.
An analysis of author's new data on characteristics of women who enter graduate school and persist in graduate study. Carefully designed to obtain a representative sample.

Davis, Natalie Z., and others. *A Study of Women Who Have Children and Who Are in Graduate Programmes at the University of Toronto.* Department of Political Economy, University of Toronto, Canada, 1966. Mimeographed.
42 of the 49 mothers in graduate programs were surveyed. Problems discussed included managing of domestic and academic duties; returning to academic discipline after some years out; financial strain; scheduling of courses at times difficult to get baby-sitters (especially in the late afternoon just before dinnertime); child-care facilities; difficulty or ease of participation in the social and intellectual community of the university; discrimination against women; and husbands' attitudes. The women surveyed recognized that many of the problems they faced were common to all graduate students and resulted from unfortunate aspects of the system of graduate study.

Farley, Jennie. "Graduate Women: Career Aspirations and Desired Family Size." *American Psychologist,* 1970(Dec),25(12), 1099-1100.
Report of a survey sponsored by a local chapter of the National Organization for Women. Half of the 263 graduate women replied that a career was "very important" in regard to all other future alternatives and were classified as career women. The other half, assigning lesser importance to a career were identified as noncareer women. Neither group appeared to anticipate much conflict between marriage and career; career women were not planning large families, although exact analysis of family size desired by both groups is not possible as item is biased. Included are comparative statistics on use of child care, husband's equal responsibility for child care and for housework.

The Fuller Utilization of the Woman Physician. Report of a Conference on Meeting Medical Manpower Needs. Sponsored by American Medical Women's Association, the President's Study Group on Careers for Women, and the Women's Bureau of the U.S. Department of Labor, January 12-13, 1968, Washington, D.C. Washington, D.C.: Women's Bureau, U.S. Department of Labor, 1968.

Conference report covers all phases of the woman physician's education and medical practical experience. Of particular interest are: John Parks, M.D., "The Medical School Years" (pp. 29-31); George A. Perera, M.D., "The Medical School Years" (pp. 63-69).

Ginzberg, Eli, and Yohalem, Alice M. *Educated American Women: Self Portraits*. New York and London: Columbia University Press, 1966.

Twenty-six narratives recount individual and personal attitudes and responses regarding the management of their lives at home and at work. Includes commentaries on graduate school attendance, its obstacles and opportunities, and increase of pressure to meet the demands of home, children, and work.

Ginzberg, Eli, and associates. *Life Styles of Educated Women*. New York and London: Columbia University Press, 1966.

Analysis of responses of more than 300 women who were graduate students between 1945 and 1951 to a 1963 questionnaire. Authors conclude that educated women do not lead constricted and discontented lives and, for the most part, are able to balance career and family satisfactorily. It has been noted, by the authors and others, that the findings may not be of general use since both the sample and the study design probably affected the findings.

Sixteen Reports on the Status of Women in the Professions. Reports presented at the Conference of Professional and Academic Women, April 11, 1970, New York University Law School. Issued in commemoration of the 50th Anniversary of the Passage of the Suffrage Amendment by the Professional Women's Caucus. Available from KNOW, INC., Box 10197, Pittsburgh, Pa. 15232.

Reports on the status of women by: Kate Millet (Academic Profession); Florence Howe (Academic Profession); Lucinda Cisler (Architecture); Sara Saporta (Art); Susan Brownmiller (Communications); Lucy Komisar (Media); Rhoda Honigman (Engineering); Sonia Pressman (Federal Government); Diana Gordon (Municipal Government); Doris L. Sassower (Law and Professions); Phyllis Wetherby (Library); L. Morrow (Medicine); Adele E. Uskali Edisen (Science); Georgia L. McMurray (Social Work); Kay Klotzburger (Professional Associations); Jan Goodman (Students); and Eleanor Holmes Norton (Organizational Challenges). These include commentaries on graduate school opportunities and obstacles in preparation for these professions.

7. Educational Behavior and Aspirations of the Mature Woman

Adult Education Association. "Continuing Education for Women: Symposium." *Adult Leadership*, 1969(May),18(1),5-36.
Collection of views on trends, problems, directions, and goals of continuing education for women. Compiled, with an introduction, by Rosalind Loring.

An Imperative for the Seventies: Releasing Creative Woman Power. A Guide for Counselors of Mature Women. St. Louis, Mo.: University of Missouri at St. Louis, Extension Division, 1969.
Compilation of conference papers delineating new directions to investigate and pursue in the education of mature women in order to utilize their creative potential.

Berry, Jane, and others. *Counseling Girls and Women: Awareness, Analysis, and Action.* Kansas City: University of Missouri at Kansas City, 1966.
A guide for employment counselors and other counselors of girls and women to assist them in establishing continuing education programs which will recognize the specialized needs of girls and women.

Buccieri, Claudia. "Continuing Education: If at First You Don't Succeed." *College and University Business*, 1970(Feb),84-86.
Part of a major section devoted to women, this article criticizes higher education's failure in the last few decades to hold women's commitment and reviews opportunities for women to renew their educational interests and goals through continuing programs of education for women. Specific programs and their particular emphases or attractions are reviewed.

Dennis, Lawrence E., ed. *Education and a Woman's Life: The Itasca Conference on the Continuing Education of Women.* Washington, D.C.: American Council on Education, 1963.
Basically a compendium of speeches and comments from the conferees; of particular interest in that opinions have not changed very much.

Dolan, Eleanor F. "Women's Continuing Education: Some National Resources." *Journal of the National Association of Women Deans and Counselors*, 1965(Fall),29(1),34-38.
Synthesis of the interest and efforts of national associations on behalf of the promotion of women's continuing education programs. Associations and programs mentioned as having made particular contributions include National Association of Women Deans and Counselors, National University Extension Association, Adult Education Association, College-Level Examination Program, and Association of University Evening Colleges.

Doty, Barbara A. "Why Do Mature Women Return to College?" *Journal of the National Association of Women Deans and Counselors*, 1966 (Summer),29(4),171-174.

A study comparing 40 mature women in baccalaureate degree programs and 40 mature women who never enrolled in higher education programs after the age of 23. Returnees were found highly motivated to manipulate their environment to meet their developmental needs; nonreturnees were uninclined to change their traditional views and, in general, had husbands whose educational motivations were not high.

Eyde, Lorraine D. "Work Motivation of Women College Graduates: Five-Year Follow-Up." *Journal of Counseling Psychology*, 1968(Mar),15(2), 199-202.

This study, based on an earlier investigation of women's desire to work (Eyde, Lorraine D., *Work Values and Background Factors as Predictors of Women's Desire to Work*. Columbus, Ohio: Ohio State University, Bureau of Business Research Monograph No. 108, 1962), explores the work motivation of two groups of college alumnae who were tested for the original study in 1958 and retested in 1963. Work motivation ratings for the 10-year alumnae were more closely related to their self-rating scores as 5-year alumnae than were the self-ratings of 5-year alumnae to their scores as college seniors. Work values of both groups showed general stability over the five-year interval except for some changes (Independence and Interesting-Variety) possibly attributable to marriage and motherhood. No decline in the value placed on mastery-achievement was shown by the 10-year alumnae when compared to the 5-year alumnae, contradictory to findings of other researchers.

Farley, Jennie. "Women Going Back to Work: Preliminary Problems." *Journal of Employment Counseling*, 1970(Dec),7(4),130-136.

Predominant preliminary problems discovered by this report are: lack of self-confidence, lack of skill in credential preparation, and, for many, the lack of sufficient self-assurance to enable them to identify themselves without reference to their marital status.

Gavron, Hannah. *The Captive Wife: Conflicts of Housebound Mothers.* London: Routledge and Kegan Paul, 1966.

Study of roles, role conflicts and role satisfactions of young British housewives with children in the home in regard to husbands' participation. Both working-class and middle-class women were included in the subject sample; findings are remarkably similar to comparable studies done in the United States — that is, Nye and Hoffman, eds., *The Employed Mother in America*.

Halfter, Irma. "The Comparative Achievement of Young and Old." *Journal of the National Association of Women Deans and Counselors*, 1962(Jan),25(2),60-67.

A study of the academic performance of older and younger women in the same undergraduate degree program in two universities revealed that the older women gave better average total performance on per course and per woman measures than did young women. On the average the older women scored 10 percentile points better than their younger classmates. Lengthy absence from formal study produced no discernible effect on academic performance; this, the author suggests, is attributable to the older women's greater scholastic motivation and willingness to spend time on studies. The author concludes that the most important finding was the superior performance (judged by any criteria) of those older women with above-average high school achievement records and a long absence from formal study.

Harmon, Lenore W. "Women's Interests — Fact or Fiction?" *Personnel and Guidance Journal*, 1967(May),45(9),895-900.
Report of an attempt to increase the number of A and B+ scores on the women's SVIB which found that the desired effect was attained by using a different item selection and weighting system from the original rather than varying the marital status of the criterion group. The author suggests that, for women, differences from a criterion group must be greater than for men if a valid vocational interest is to be measured.

Hembrough, Betty L. "A Two-Fold Educational Challenge: The Student Wife and the Mature Woman Student." *Journal of the National Association of Women Deans and Counselors*, 1966(Summer),29(4),163-167.
Based on findings of a 1962-63 survey at the University of Illinois, this article discusses barriers to educational opportunity for student wives and mature women (for example, course scheduling, lack of day-care centers, library resources, counseling services, financial aid).

Hiltunen, Wandalyn Axthelm. "A Counseling Course for the Mature Woman." *Journal of the National Association of Women Deans and Counselors*, 1968(Winter),31(2),93-96.
Description of one year's service of a trial evening counseling course for women.

***Implications of Women's Work Patterns for Vocational and Technical Education.* Research Series No. 19. Columbus, Ohio: Center for Vocational and Technical Education, Ohio State University, 1967.**
Report of a work conference attended by 30 representatives of various services in vocational and technical education to examine women's work patterns (occupations, participation rate, educational attainment, reasons for unemployment) and personal characteristics (marital status, age, race, number of children) of these women and to assess implications of these statistics for future directions of vocational and technical education; copious statistical figures.

Johnstone, John W. C., and Rivera, Ramon J. *Volunteers for Learning: A*

Study of the Educational Pursuits of American Adults. National Opinion Research Center, Monographs in Social Research. Chicago: Aldine Publishing Company, 1965.

Most detailed study to date of the clientele in continuing or adult education including statistics on differences in the participation patterns of men and women. Males are more apt than females to participate in continuing education with a vocational orientation and in degree programs.

Knowles, Malcolm S. *The Adult Education Movement in the United States.* New York: Holt, Rinehart and Winston, 1962.

History of the adult education movement in the United States from the eighteenth century to the present, with an analysis of current and future trends.

Leland, Carole. "Structures and Strangers in Higher Education," in *An Imperative for the Seventies: Releasing Creative Woman Power.* St. Louis, Mo.: University of Missouri at St. Louis, Extension Division, 1969, pp. 15-18.

Critical review of the growth of continuing education for women in the 1960s and suggested response actions (including use of the College-Level Examination Program) for institutions to consider in meeting the needs of mature women.

Letchworth, George E. "Women Who Return to College: An Identity-Integrity Approach." *Journal of College Student Personnel,* 1970(Mar), 11(2),103-106.

Examination of motivations and adjustment difficulties of older women re-entering higher education.

Likert, Jane Gibson, ed. *Conversations with Returning Women Students.* Ann Arbor: Center for Continuing Education, University of Michigan, 1967.

Synthesis of a 1967 conversation-discussion series under the Center's auspices on the theme of "Women in School and Work"; descriptive of actual experiences in dealing with finances, fear of failure, husbands' attitudes, incidents of discrimination, management ability in home and work, and other problems returning women students face.

Matthews, Esther E. "The Counselor and the Adult Woman." *Journal of the National Association of Women Deans and Counselors,* 1969 (Spring), 32(3),115-122.

A proposal for an 8-phase counseling plan to aid in the personal and vocational development of women in modern suburbia. The eight phases: Inner Preparation; Intensive Family Involvement; Vocational Experimentation; Vocational Planning; Vocational Implementation; Vocational Analysis; Vocational Resynthesis; and Vocational Development Resource.

McMillan, Sylvia R. "Aspirations of Low-Income Mothers." *Journal of Marriage and the Family,* 1967(May),29(2),282-287.
Personal interviews with 32 low-income mothers from urban and rural areas indicate dissatisfaction with their present conditions and aspirations that are not unrealistic. The women indicate a desire for more education for themselves if it will lead to a good paying job. For their daughters, their aspirations include marriage, home and family, and "as much education as they (the daughters) can get."

Merideth, Elizabeth, and Merideth, Robert. "Adult Women's Education: A Radical Critique." *Journal of the National Association of Women Deans and Counselors,* 1971(Spring),34(3),111-120.
Urges that reform in adult education for women depends on radical changes in the system including: deans of women who are radical feminists; increased employment of married women on the university's professional staff; development of a model community within the university which stresses the "non-oppressive, fulfilling, productive humane life"; encouragement of nepotism; provision of day-care services for all segments of the university community; wide options in living arrangements including coed, co-op, and single sex dormitories, apartments, and houses for all segments of the university community; formal and informal approaches to women's studies; and elimination of sex-role stereotyping in career guidance.

Parrish, John B. "Coming Crisis in Women's Higher Education and Work." AAUW *Journal,* 1970(Nov),17-19.
An analysis of the credibility gap between higher education and women's work; the author presents a restructuring plan for both areas to offset an otherwise predictable widening gap in the 1970s.

Raines, Max. *An Appraisal of the New York State Guidance Center for Women.* Albany: State University of New York, 1970.
An evaluation of the first state-supported guidance center for women during its pilot-project period. Indicates strengths as well as weaknesses of this specialized service from which those considering initiation of such a center can benefit. A major finding was that 87 percent of the random sample of clients interviewed by the evaluating team believed the Center's services had a positive impact on their lives.

Schletzer, Vera M.; Cless, Elizabeth L.; McCune, Cornelia W.; Mantini, Barbara K.; and Loeffler, Dorothy L. *A Five-Year Report 1960-65 of Minnesota Plan for the Continuing Education of Women.* Minneapolis: University of Minnesota, 1967.
Description of the development, clientele, counseling program, curricular offerings, job placement, undergraduate program, and supporting services of a continuing education program for women at the University of Minnesota; one of the first services to women of its kind.

Stern, Bernard H., and Missal, Ellsworth. *Adult Experience and College Degrees.* Cleveland: Press of Western Reserve University, 1960.
Report of experimental degree program at Brooklyn College in late 1950s that used examinations and seminars to give credit for experience and to accelerate the acquisition of credit. (The program is still operating.)

U. S. Department of Labor, Wage and Standards Administration, Women's Bureau. *Continuing Education Programs and Services for Women.* Revised, and including bibliography on continuing education for women. Washington, D.C.: Women's Bureau, Spring 1971.
An identification of courses and services offered by almost 450 institutions and organizations; includes a list of related programs for which federal funds have been awarded.

Washington, Bennetta B. "Education in League with the Future: Job Corps." *Journal of the National Association of Women Deans and Counselors,* 1966(Summer),29(4),184-187.
Drawing upon her experience as Director of Job Corps Centers for Women, the author cites community support of and participation in educational programs as the key to the personal, educational, and vocational development of the impoverished.

Westervelt, Esther M. "New Feminists and Suburban Housewives: Allies or Opponents?," in Katz, Joseph; Comstock, Margaret, et al. *The Quest for Autonomy in Adult Women* (working title). New York: Van Nostrand Reinhold Co. (In press.)
Analysis of suburban women indicating that, in general, they do not subscribe to feminist goals and that their attitudes and aspirations are not those of feminists.

Westervelt, Esther M. *Releasing Women's Potentialities: The Two-Year College as Catalyst.* Albany: State University of New York, 1969.
Proceedings of a conference held for representatives of two-year colleges in the State University of New York system to familiarize them with issues and resources for the establishment of programs and services for the mature woman, and to explore new ideas for future development.

Westervelt, Esther M. "Education, Vocation and Avocation in Women's Lives," in Scott, Anne Firor, ed., *What Is Happening to American Women.* Atlanta, Ga.: Southern Newspapers Publishers Association Foundation, 1970, pp. 67-93.
Review of the development of continuing education for women, especially during the past 15 years, discussion of some psychological and social characteristics of women who tend to be in these programs, and recommendations for new approaches. Emphasizes that, to date, continuing education has served primarily middle-class women.

8. Women and Employment

Astin, Helen S. *The Woman Doctorate in America*. New York: Russell
   Sage Foundation, 1969.
Large-scale statistical research survey of women in the United States receiving doctoral degrees in 1957 and 1958; examines career commitment and
interruption, personal and family characteristics of women doctorates, their
career development, employment patterns, achievements, and rewards.

Baetjer, Anne M. "Health Problems Among Employed Women." *Journal
   of the National Association of Women Deans and Counselors*. 1966
   (Summer),29(4),156-159.
Concise summary of then-current health data and industrial practice; statistics indicate women's health risk liability is no greater than that of men.

Baker, Elizabeth Faulkner. *Technology and Woman's Work*. New York:
   Columbia University Press, 1964.
Historical rather than predictive exploration of the impact of industrial technology on women's labor force participation and, concomitantly on the employment patterns of those women in the lower echelons of the labor force;
examines twentieth century trends and forces, including the role of the unions.

Banks, Ann. "Present Company Excepted." *Brown Alumni Monthly*,
   1971(Jan),71(4),18-23.
Somewhat informal report on women's academic status; emphasis on Brown
graduates.

Baruch, Rhoda Wasserman. "The Achievement Motive in Women: Implications for Career Development." *Journal of Personality and Social
   Psychology*, 1967(Sep),5(3),260-267.
Report of a study testing two hypotheses: (1) there is a temporal cycle in need
for achievement associated with age and family situation; and (2) high Need-
Achievement is associated with return to paid employment. Data from TAT
stories written by 137 Radcliffe alumnae supported the hypotheses. A broader
test with a nationwide sample of 763 women failed to confirm either hypothesis. The first relationship obtained for the college women in the sample. Further analysis indicated that there was a time lag between increased Need-
Achievement and increased participation in paid employment.

Bernard, Jessie. *Academic Women*. University Park, Pa.: Pennsylvania
   State University Press, 1964.
Study of women employed in academic field presents modal description of
the subjects who, according to statistics, tend to permit teaching commitments to take preference over research commitments, to be compliant, to

remain at elementary levels of instruction, and to be less anxious than men to pursue graduate study.

Berry, Jane; McCarty, Edward R.; Bates, Jean M.; and Terrill, Hazel J. *Guide for Development of Permanent Part-Time Employment Opportunities for Girls and Women.* Prepared for the Missouri Department of Labor and Industrial Relations. Kansas City, Mo.: University of Missouri at Kansas City, 1969.
Guide reinforces need for part-time job consciousness at managerial levels; includes specific information in areas where such employment can be found as well as several case histories.

Bock, E. Wilbur. "The Female Clergy: A Case of Professional Marginality." *American Journal of Sociology,* 1967(Mar),72(5),531-539.
Extensively documented study concludes that the status given women in the clergy can scarcely be termed professional.

Bowman, Garda W.; Worthy, N. Beatrice; and Greyser, Stephen A. "Are Women Executives People? Survey of Attitudes of 2,000 Executives." *Harvard Business Review,* 1965(Jul-Aug),43(4),14ff.
Substantial article reporting the attitudes of 1,000 male and 1,000 female executives on sex equality in employment, opportunities for and acceptance of female executives, actions to correct inequities; more than 80 percent of all respondents think that the law's administration, rather than its provisions, will determine the impact of the Civil Rights Act, and most opt for voluntary action to help achieve equality of opportunity for women. Both men and women interviewed agreed that the female executive has to be overqualified.

Business and Professional Women's Foundation. *Profile of Business and Professional Women.* Washington, D.C.: Business and Professional Women's Foundation, 1970.
Study of members of the National Federation of Business and Professional Women's Clubs provides statistical information, based on more than 53,000 responses, on occupations, incomes, age, education, marital, and professional status.

Cain, Glen G. *Married Women in the Labor Force: An Economic Analysis.* Chicago: University of Chicago Press, 1967.
A statistical presentation of economic, educational, family and racial variables that affect women's participation in the labor force. Findings on the effects of these variables on labor force behavior in women are similar to those in other studies; level of education, membership in a nonwhite racial group, and absence of preschool children in the home all correlate positively with labor force participation. However, the presence and ages of children appear to be decreasing in effect in recent years.

Discrimination against Women. Hearings before the Special Subcommittee of the Committee on Education and Labor, House of Representatives, Ninety-first Congress, Second Session on Section 805 of H.R. 16098. Hearings Held in Washington June 17, 19, and 30, 1970 (Part I) and July 1 and 31, 1970 (Part II). Washington, D.C.: Government Printing Office, 1970.

Of inestimable value in assessment of modern employment practices affecting women. Contains reports on discrimination against women from an extremely wide variety of qualified sources.

Doty, Barbara A. "Study of Characteristics of Women Who Begin Teaching after Age 35." *Industrial Gerontology*, 1971(Winter),52-54.

This study, using GPA and college entrance test scores as measures, finds that older women teachers (35 to 45 years of age) surpass younger (21-24) counterparts in achievement, adjustment, and ability to teach effectively. It also appeared that the best predictor of teacher effectiveness was the negative criticism of critic teachers; age differential may be a factor in the negative attitude of the, usually, younger critic teachers.

Epstein, Cynthia. *Woman's Place: Options and Limits in Professional Careers.* Berkeley: University of California Press, 1970.

Beginning with a survey of cultural themes, value systems, socialization and role conflict, this book focuses on the structure, behavior norms, and tendencies to change on the part of particular professions as they relate to the women in them, effects of these on women at all levels of the work force; based on data drawn from the professions.

The "Equal Rights" Amendment: Hearings before the Subcommittee on Constitutional Amendments of the Committee on the Judiciary, U.S. Senate, 91st Congress, 2nd Session, on S.J. Res. 61. Washington, D.C.: Government Printing Office, 1970.

Equal Rights 1970: Hearings before the Committee on the Judiciary, U.S. Senate, 91st Congress, 2nd Session on S.J. Res. 61 and S.J. Res. 231. Washington, D.C.: Government Printing Office, 1970.

Eyde, Lorraine D. "Eliminating Barriers to Career Development of Women." *Personnel and Guidance Journal,* 1970(Sep),49(1),24-28.

Well-documented proposal for increased vocational guidance, especially for girls from the upper-middle class (data indicate these to be the major source of women Ph.D.'s) and for low-income mothers, the prospective New Careers participants.

Gould, Jane Schwartz. "Discrimination in Employment." *Barnard Alumnae,* 1970(Spring),59(3),29-30.

Drawing upon concrete examples, this women's college placement director cites incidents of employment discrimination against women in company literature, interviews, job listings, and promotional opportunities.

Graham, Patricia Albjerg. *"Women in Academe."* Science, 1970(Sep23), 169,1284-1290.
An historical review and analysis of the current situation of women in academic employment, the reasons for it, and corrective measures that should be taken.

Harmon, Lenore W. "Women's Working Patterns Related to Their SVIB Housewife and 'Own' Occupational Scores." *Journal of Counseling Psychology*, 1967(Jul),14(4),299-301.
The hypothesis for this study was that women who had remained in a career for the greater portion of the 25 years since taking the SVIB would have had lower Housewife scores than those women who had placed the responsibilities of home and family before those of a career. Results, however, show that none of the career women (subdivided into five groups according to career commitment) differed much from the marriage/family oriented women on the Housewife scale; all, 25 years ago, had scored in the B and B— range. Career women also determined their own scores as they would be derived from the SVIB; only in the case of Career Group 5 (those who had worked continuously since leaving undergraduate school) was support for the hypothesis found.

Harmon, Lenore W., and Campbell, David P. "Use of Interest Inventories with Nonprofessional Women: Stewardesses versus Dental Assistants." *Journal of Counseling Psychology*, 1968(Jan),15(1),17-22.
Study to determine measurable vocational interest differences of stewardesses and dental assistants, all purported to be happy with their jobs. SVIB scores were compared with SVIB scores of Women-in-General (Strong's W-I-G group, heavily weighted with professional women); results show measurable differences not only between the nonprofessional women and the W-I-G group, but also between the two groups of nonprofessionals. Results lead authors to accept feasibility of measuring vocational interests of other nonprofessionals and to propose that knowledge gained will free women to choose employment on interest factors rather than job level.

Hennig, Margaret. *Career Development for Women Executives.* Doctoral Dissertation, Harvard Graduate School of Business Administration, 1971. Unpublished.
Doctoral study, reported in the press, of 35 career women; common personal characteristics and career crises (most noteworthy occurs around age 35) are revealed in this research study of 35 top-level women executives. Further information may be obtained from the author: Dr. Margaret Hennig, Associate Professor of Management and Organizational Behavior, Simmons College, Boston, Massachusetts.

Katelman, D. K., and Barnett, L. D. "Work Orientations of Urban, Middle-Class, Married Women." *Journal of Marriage and the Family*, 1968 (Feb),30(1),80-88.

Well-organized investigation of characteristics that differentiate positive and negative attitudes in married women toward the employment of wives and mothers; age and husband's education are two differentiating variables.

Keniston, Kenneth, and Keniston, Ellen. "An American Anachronism: The Image of Women and Work." *The American Scholar,* **1964(Summer),33(3),355-375.**
The authors contend that American stereotypes of femininity are antithetical to strong career commitments in women. They believe that a change in this condition is dependent on changes in the role models available to girls and in psychiatric conceptions of the mentally healthy female, as well as on active efforts in the educational and employment sectors to increase career opportunities for women.

King, Alice Gore. *Help Wanted: Female.* **New York: Charles Scribner's Sons, 1968.**
Informative guide to jobs for newcomers to the labor force and to changing opportunities for the mature woman.

Klein, Viola. *Women Workers: Working Hours and Services, A Survey in Twenty-One Countries.* **Paris: Organization for Economic Cooperation and Development, 1965.**
Gives data on working hours in industry, administrative work, distributive trades, and services; community services for working women with family responsibilities; special arrangements for expectant mothers and those with infants; opening and closing times of shops, post offices, local administrative offices, and so forth, in relation to working hours.

Lamson, Peggy. *Few Are Chosen: American Women in Political Life Today.* **Boston: Houghton Mifflin Co., 1968.**
Biographies of women political officeholders implement author's examination of obstacles for women in this field.

Lembeck, Ruth. *380 Part-Time Jobs for Women.* **New York: Dell, 1969.**
A guide to part-time employment, with informational assistance to the beginner.

Levinson, Perry. "How Employable Are AFDC Women?" U.S. Department of Health, Education, and Welfare, Social and Rehabilitation Service, *Welfare in Review,* **1970(Jul-Aug),8(4),12-16.**
Study report reveals waste in employment potential of AFDC women in that the rise of employment potential in women receiving aid for dependent children has been offset by a greater rise of employment barriers (more so than for AFDC women with low employment potential) over the period 1961-1968.

Mattfield, Jacquelyn A., and Van Aken, Carol G., eds. *Women and the Scientific Professions.* **Cambridge, Mass.: Massachusetts Institute of Technology Press, 1965.**

Collection of essays on women's status and opportunities within the scientific fields.

Morsink, Helen M. "Leader Behavior of Men and Women Secondary School Principals." *Educational Horizons*, 1968-69(Winter),47(2),69-74.
A report of faculty evaluations of 15 secondary school principals of each sex in terms of 12 selected "dimensions of leader-behavior"; data analyzed collectively and by sex of the teacher-respondents. The women teachers perceived no significant differences between male and female principals on six leader behaviors; on the remaining six, they perceived female principals as excercising these behaviors to a greater degree. The male teachers rated male principals higher than female principals on only one dimension — Tolerance of Freedom; on three dimensions, they perceived the male and female principals as equal; on eight dimensions, they perceived female principals to show these behaviors to a greater extent. Findings indicate no valid reasons for the general failure to employ women in this role.

National Manpower Council. *Womanpower*. New York: Columbia University Press, 1957.
Analysis of the female labor force in the late 1950s with predictions of future trends and recommendations for needed related services. A major study in its time; of historical interest now.

National Manpower Council. *Work in the Lives of Married Women*. New York: Columbia University Press, 1958.
Includes chapters by separate authors on the following topics: education and guidance of women for reentry into the labor force; utilization of women workers over 35; incomes earned by married women; development of the children of working mothers.

Nochlin, Linda. "Why Have There Been No Great Women Artists?" *Artnews*, 1971(Jan),69(9),22-39 and ff.
A scholarly, tightly reasoned explanation of the reasons there have been few great women artists. Through a review of the backgrounds and careers of the best-known women artists of the past few centuries, the author documents the negative effects of both socialization and lack of opportunity for training upon artistic creativity in women.

Nye, F. Ivan, and Hoffman, Lois Wladis, eds. *The Employed Mother in America*. Chicago: Rand McNally, 1963.
A collection and a review of significant sociological and sociopsychological research conducted from 1957 to the cut-off date early in 1962. Includes research on: the social, economic, sociopsychological, and psychological differences between mothers in and outside the labor force; the children of employed and nonemployed mothers; the marital relationships of employed and nonemployed mothers; and the comparison of self-feelings, health, and relationships of the two categories of women.

Oltman, Ruth M. *Campus 1970: Where Do Women Stand?* Research Report of a Survey on Women in Academe. Washington, D.C.: American Association of University Women, 1970.

Report of a survey of the academic status of women at all levels. Questionnaire findings confirm other data indicating that women students, administrators, faculty, and trustees are underrepresented in numbers and in decision-making authority. The evaluation covers: for the student — positions of leadership, programs for women, participation on student-staff committees, residence, pregnancy and birth control policies, and enrollment of mature women students; for women administrators — policy-making structures, types of administrative positions, and hiring policies; for the faculty women — department chairmanship, maternity leave policies, extent of representation, and nepotism policies; and for the woman trustee — representation on the top governing board. Findings also indicate that practice and policy with regard to women were not compatible. One-third of the 750 colleges and universities queried did not respond, a fact which, the author suggests, could indicate a greater extent of negative attitudes than the data presented reveal.

O'Neill, Barbara Powell. *Careers for Women after Marriage and Children.* New York: Macmillan, 1965.

A substantial handbook (286 pp.) giving advice on continuing education, on "traditional" women's careers (health, social work, teaching, and so forth), and on some more "pioneering" ones (engineering, city planning, and so forth). Brief career histories of mature women who entered these fields, including their comments on raising children while pursuing their career and some examples of their daily schedules.

Oppenheimer, Valerie Kincade. *The Female Labor Force in the United States: Factors Governing Its Growth and Changing Composition.* Berkeley: Institute of International Studies, University of California, 1970.

While the demand for female labor has been increasing, the supply has fluctuated in a complicated way. Although the female labor force as a whole has been expanding, women who used to provide the backbone of the female labor force (for example, the unmarried and the young) constituted a stationary or declining population group in the period from 1940 to 1960. The only way a rising demand for female labor force could have been met is by the increased employment of older, married women. The author summarizes data on increased opportunity for such women in certain areas and stresses the influence of demand or opportunity on women's decisions to enter or leave the labor force, as opposed to psychological factors or factors such as changes in homemaking conditions.

Rossi, Alice. "Discrimination and Demography Restrict Opportunities for Academic Women." *College and University Business*, 1970(Feb),74-78.

Statistical review of the status of women in American institutions of higher education over the past three decades and the author's perspective on future trends; the author attributes the recent increase in the participation of older women in the work force to the low birth rates of the 1930s and predicts for the 1970s an increase in participation by the young and childless woman and continued discrimination if employers remain unable to distinguish career women as individuals and not as facsimiles of their homemaker-wives or usurpers of economic benefits.

Rossi, Alice. "Women in Science: Why So Few?" *Science*, 1965(May28), 148,1196-1202.
Over the period 1950-1960, the rate of increase of women employed in science and engineering was 209 percent, compared to a rate among men of 428 percent. Women working in these fields are less likely than men to have advanced degrees, less likely to be employed in industry, and less likely to be married. They earn less money than men and work fewer hours per week. This paper includes a brief review of recent work on cognitive differences between males and females. The author cites male conservatism as one force that may be hindering women, particularly scientists, in their professional development. She sees the increasingly common pattern of intermittent careers for women as a counter-revolutionary force, tending to perpetuate women's lower achievement in the professions. Older women can be retrained for lower positions, but only rarely as doctors, full-fledged scientists, or engineers. The author cites with approval recent trends in the discussion of working mothers, trends that argue for the establishment of child-care centers and for the cognitive stimulation a child may possibly receive from a working mother.

Schramm, Dwayne Gene. "A Study of the Older Woman Worker Who Has Attempted to Re-Enter the White Collar Labor Force through Assistance of Community Training Programs in Clerical Occupations." *Industrial Gerontology*, 1971(Winter),47-48.
Profile of the modal woman reentering the labor force through clerical training programs.

Scobey, J., and McGrath, Lee P. *Creative Careers for Women: A Handbook of Sources and Ideas for Part-Time Jobs.* New York: Simon and Schuster, 1968.
Guide covering self-employment and employment in various areas of business, industry, and the professions for various age groups.

Siegel, Alberta E., and Curtis, Elizabeth. "Familial Correlates of Orientation toward Future Employment among College Women." *Journal of Educational Psychology*, 1963(Feb),54(1),33-37.
Information obtained by interviewers of 43 young women (random sample of sophomore women at a large university) was coded by two independent scalers to determine measures of the work orientation of the subjects and

five characteristics. Of the five characteristics (SES, parents' educational level, mother's work orientation, parents' views on the purpose of college, and parents' attitudes toward the importance of education for the daughter), only mother's work orientation was found to be of significant correlation with work orientation of the subjects. Most subjects stated that they aspired to marriage and employment. Sample may have been too homogeneous to expose other correlations, the authors suggest.

Simon, Rita J.; Clark, Shirley M.; and Gallway, K. "The Woman Ph.D.: A Recent Profile." *Social Problems*, 1967(Fall),15(2),221-236.
A study describing the professional characteristics of women who received their Ph.D.'s in four major academic divisions between the years 1958 and 1963, and who are employed full time. Compared with men who received Ph.D.'s in the same areas at the same times in such aspects as type and place of employment, professorial rank, tenure, salaries, productivity (publications), and professional recognition, women are less likely, especially in education, to receive administrative posts, to receive equal salaries or promotional opportunities; in two measures (of three), however, of professional recognition, women did proportionately better than men. More than 95 percent of the men in the study were married; only 50 percent of the women were married.

Simpson, Lawrence A. "A Myth is Better Than a Miss: Men Get the Edge in Academic Employment." *College and University Business*, 1970 (Feb),72-73.
Report of a 1968 study, encompassing six Pennsylvania colleges, indicates that, all other variables being equal, male candidates are typically chosen over female candidates for employment.

Smuts, Robert W. *Women and Work in America.* New York: Columbia University Press, 1959.
An historical summary, covering the late nineteenth century to the present; with particular emphasis on changing attitudes.

U.S. Civil Service Commission, Bureau of Management Services. *Study of Employment of Women in the Federal Government*, 1968. Prepared for the Federal Women's Program. Washington, D.C.: Government Printing Office, 1969.
Comparison of the status of federally employed women with that of the total full-time white-collar government work force.

U.S. Department of Labor, Bureau of Labor Statistics. *Occupational Employment Patterns for 1960 and 1975.* Bulletin #1599. Washington, D.C.: Government Printing Office, December 1968.
Extensive data on employment projections in all areas, supplemented with 1960 data on labor force composition and trends; compiled for state governments to assist in manpower training program planning.

U.S. Department of Labor, Bureau of Labor Statistics. *Women and the Labor Force.* Special Labor Force Report No. 93. Reprinted from *Monthly Labor Review,* February 1970 (reprint No. 2560).

Married women now constitute 20 percent of the labor force. Increase in number has not been accompanied by material wage improvement over the last several years.

U.S. Department of Labor, Manpower Administration. "Women Professional Workers," in *Manpower Demand and Supply in Professional Occupations,* a chapter reprint from *1970 Manpower Report of the President.* Washington, D.C.: Government Printing Office, 1970, pp. 185-189.

Discussion of the probable shift in women's professional employment patterns due to the changing supply-and-demand situation in the traditional "women's professions," as well as to the increasing number of women seeking a college education.

U.S. Department of Labor, Wage and Labor Standards Administration, Women's Bureau. *Automation and Women Workers.* Washington, D.C.: Women's Bureau, February 1970.

Implications of technological progress in women's employment and their working conditions. Employment data for 1958-1968 reveal that some barriers have been removed (inroads into "men's work") and that skill levels have increased.

U.S. Department of Labor, Wage and Labor Standards Administration, Women's Bureau. *Background Facts on Women Workers in the United States.* Washington, D.C.: Women's Bureau, 1968.

Statistical summary of labor force and demographic characteristics of women workers.

U.S. Department of Labor, Wage and Labor Standards Administration, Women's Bureau. *Facts about Women's Absenteeism and Labor Turnover.* Washington, D.C.: Women's Bureau, August 1969.

Women workers' attendance at work and labor turnover compare favorably with those of men when job levels and such circumstances as skill level of job, age, length of service, and personal record of job stability are similar. Absenteeism and turnover are associated with these factors rather than with sex.

U.S. Department of Labor, Wage and Labor Standards Administration, Women's Bureau. *Fact Sheet on the Earnings Gap.* Washington, D.C.: Government Printing Office, 1970.

Data on wage and salary income for men and women. Especially noteworthy among the statistics is the decline of women's median income, as a percentage of men's, in full-time year-round employment over the years 1955 to 1967.

U.S. Department of Labor, Wage and Labor Standards Administration, Women's Bureau. *Negro Women in the Population and Labor Force.* Washington, D.C.: Government Printing Office, 1968.
A statistical description of the Negro woman in the work force, her educational attainment, wage and salary income, contribution to family income, employment status, and child-care arrangements.

U.S. Department of Labor, Wage and Labor Standards Administration, Women's Bureau. *1969 Handbook on Women Workers.* Washington, D.C.: Government Printing Office, 1969.
Complete statistical information on women in the labor force: participation and characteristics; occupations and employment patterns; education and training; federal and state laws affecting women in these areas. Excellent bibliography on "American Women Workers."

U.S. Department of Labor, Wage and Labor Standards Administration, Women's Bureau. *Summary of State Labor Laws for Women.* Washington, D.C.: Government Printing Office, March 1969.
Reports principal standards and employment regulations of the 50 states, the District of Columbia, and Puerto Rico applicable to women with regard to minimum wage, fair employment practices, work hours, equal pay, and overtime.

U.S. Department of Labor, Wage and Labor Standards Administration, Women's Bureau. *Underutilization of Women Workers.* Washington, D.C.: Government Printing Office. Revised, 1971.
Description of the underutilization of women workers in relation to educational achievement, unemployment, employment in low-skilled jobs, and the earnings differential.

U.S. Department of Labor, Wage and Labor Standards Administration, Women's Bureau. *Women Workers Today.* (WB70-211) Washington, D.C.: Government Printing Office, 1970.
Survey of personal and employment characteristics of 31 million women in the labor force today.

U.S. Department of Labor, Wage and Labor Standards Administration, Women's Bureau. *Working Wives — Their Contribution to Family Income.* Washington, D.C.: Government Printing Office, November 1968.
Statistics covering 1965-66, for the most part, on working women's contribution to the family's economic resources.

White, James J. "Women in the Law." *Michigan Law Review,* 1967, 65(B), 1051-1122.
Comparative study of women lawyers and a matched male sample to determine differences in employment sphere, opportunities, and experience, and to delineate extent of sex discrimination. The subjects were studied with

regard to: earnings, job profiles, career patterns, work performed, family factors, attitudes and opinions on sex discrimination, and motives for studying law. Sex discrimination is analyzed by the author in terms of class rank and law review, school attended, type of employer, type of work performed and of job sought, validity of male sample, evidence of discrimination, and possible variables affecting discrimination (intelligence, emotional stability, probable length of service, client confidence). Findings include: women more than men find long-term employment in government; men have higher starting salaries and faster increases than do women lawyers; examination of family background and situation variables uncovered no significant differences between the sexes; 50 percent of the women said they had experienced sex discrimination, 17 percent said they probably had; 94 percent of the women said they would do it all over again.

White, Kinnard. "Social Background Variables Related to Career Commitment of Women Teachers." *Personnel and Guidance Journal*, 1967 (Mar),45(7),648-652.
Study findings suggest that differential in career commitment among women teachers is determined by certain social background factors: mother's work orientation, social class, source of financial support for college, and current marital status. Type of college does not appear to be a differentiating variable.

White, Martha S. "Psychological and Social Barriers to Women in Science." *Science.* 1970(Oct),170(3956),413-416.
Discussion of the effect of women's advancement in scientific fields of career interruptions, lack of part-time employment opportunities, exclusion from informal channels of communication among scientists, difficulty in finding sponsors, and inadequate socialization because of lack of full acceptance by peers, senior scientists, and institutions.

White, Martha S., ed. *The Next Step: A Guide to Part-Time Opportunities in Greater Boston for the Educated Woman.* Cambridge, Mass.: Radcliffe Institute for Independent Study, 1964.
An introductory essay explores the situation of the mature woman who wants new opportunities for learning, working, or community service; the essay is followed by detailed information about schools, employment possibilities, and volunteer opportunities in the Boston area. A worksheet, in the form of an open-ended questionnaire, is provided to help a woman evaluate her own possible "next step," considering her family situation, her competencies, and her conflicts.

Whitney, Mary E. "Women Student Personnel Administrators: The Past and the Future." *Journal of College Student Personnel*, 1971(Jan),12(1), 7-10.
Appraising trends by comparing past patterns of employment of women in student personnel administration with current and emerging ones, the author

raises questions about the status of women student personnel administrators in present administrative structures and about women's future in the field.

Wolfe, Helen Bickel. "An Analysis of the Work Values of Women: Implications for Counseling." *Journal of the National Association of Women Deans and Counselors,* **1969(Fall),33(1),13-17.**
More than 1,800 usable replies to a questionnaire designed to study women's work values indicated that all women valued highly the mastery, or achievement provided by work, and the social aspects of employment; this was true regardless of marital status, age, educational attainment, current employment status, career pattern, socioeconomic class, or field of work. It was found that the value placed on mastery, dominance, and economic work values can be predicted by field of work; the value of interesting activity can be predicted from educational attainment and work pattern. Other findings include: married women, as compared with divorced, widowed, separated, or unmarried women, placed the most value on mastery-achievement and had the highest expectations that work be interesting; the oldest women displayed the greatest need for independence and the highest expectation for social rewards from work; women with less education placed higher value on independence whereas women with the most education expected the greatest social rewards from work; and, women who were employed part-time had higher expectations that work would be interesting than women in full-time employment. Extrinsic rewards seemed to become more dominant if a woman had less education or held a job requiring less skill.

Wolfe, Helen Bickel. *Women in the World of Work.* **Albany, N. Y.: State University of New York, State Education Department, 1969.**
The full report of the study cited above.

"Woman's Place in the Work Force." *Issues in Industrial Society,* **1970, 2(1).**
Collection of articles on women's employment status; authors include Jessie Bernard and Elizabeth Duncan Koontz.

9. Bibliographies on Related Topics

A. On the Education and Continuing Education of Women

ERIC Clearinghouse on Adult Education. *Continuing Education of Women, Current Information Sources No. 22* (December 1968) and *Continuing Education of Women, Current Information Sources No. 32* (Sep 1970). Syracuse, N. Y.: ERIC Clearinghouse on Adult Education.

Greater Miami Council for the Continuing Education of Women. *Some Current Readings in Continuing Education for Women.* Compiled for the 1969 Atlanta Convention of the National Association of Women Deans and Counselors. Miami, Fla.: Miami-Dade Junior College, April 1969. Addenda, December 1969.

Spiegel, Jeanne, ed. *A Selected Annotated Bibliography — Continuing Education for Women.* Washington, D.C.: Business and Professional Women's Foundation, 1967.

U.S. Department of Health, Education, and Welfare. Office of Education, International Organizations. *The United States of America — Equality of Access of Women and Girls to Education, 1959-1969.*
Prepared for the Bulletin of the International Bureau of Education, 1970.

U.S. Department of Labor, Wage and Labor Standards Administration, Women's Bureau. *Continuing Education Programs for Women.* Washington, D.C.: Women's Bureau. Revised, 1971.

B. On Women in the Labor Force

Business and Professional Women's Foundation. *A Selected Annotated Bibliography — Women Executives.* Washington, D.C.: Business and Professional Women's Foundation, 1970.

Hastings College of Law. *Women — The Legal and Economic Aspects of Employment — A Bibliography.* San Francisco, California: Hastings College of Law, 1969.

U.S. Department of Labor, Wage and Labor Standards Administration, Women's Bureau. *Publications of the Women's Bureau Currently Available.* Washington, D.C.: Women's Bureau, Leaflet #10, constantly revised.

U.S. Department of Labor, Wage and Labor Standards Administration, Women's Bureau. *1969 Handbook on Women Workers.* Women's Bureau Bulletin No. 294. Washington, D.C.: Government Printing Office, 1969.
Excellent bibliography on "American Women Workers."

C. General, Multifaceted, or Specialized

Astin, Helen S. *The Woman Doctorate in America*. New York: Russell Sage Foundation, 1969.
See bibliography for references on development of career orientation in girls and young women.

Bruemmer, Linda. "The Condition of Women in Society Today: Annotated Bibliography—Part II." *Journal of the National Association of Women Deans and Counselors*, 1970(Winter),33(2),89-95.

Cisler, Lucinda. *Women: A Bibliography*.
Constantly updated by the author. For information concerning costs and availability, write the author at 102 West 80th Street, New York, N. Y. 10024.

Coelho, George V.; Hamburg, David A.; Moos, Rudolph; and Randolph, Peter, eds. *Coping and Adaptation: A Behavioral Sciences Bibliography*. National Institute of Mental Health; United States Department of Health, Education, and Welfare, Public Health Service, Health Service and Mental Health Administration. Washington, D.C.: Government Printing Office, 1970.

Feminists on Children's Media. *Little Miss Muffet Fights Back: Recommended Non-Sexist Books about Girls for Young Readers*. New York: Feminist on Children's Media, Box 4315, Grand Central Station, New York, 10017. 1971.
While this does not pertain directly to higher or continuing education, it may be of interest to those who are teaching teachers.

Howe, Florence. *Female Studies II*. Pittsburgh, Pa.: KNOW, INC.
A collection of college syllabi and reading lists compiled by the Commission on the Status of Women of the Modern Language Association. Undated; includes 1971 course material.

Keiffer, Miriam G., and Warren, Patricia A. *Population Limitation and Women's Status*. Princeton, N. J.: Educational Testing Service, 1970.
Not to be cited as a published report without the specific permission of the authors. Gratitude is expressed to the authors for granting permission in this instance.

National Council on Family Relations. *Annotated Bibliography, Family Life: Literature and Films*. 1970. Available from the Minnesota Council on Family Relations, 1219 University Avenue Southeast, Minneapolis, Minn. 55414.

Oetzel, Roberta M. "Annotated Bibliography," in Maccoby, Eleanor E., ed., *The Development of Sex Differences*. Stanford, Calif.: Stanford University Press, 1966, pp. 223-321.
Bibliography of research in sex differences.

Radcliffe Institute. *Womanpower: Selected Bibliography on Educated Women and the Labor Force.* Cambridge, Mass.: Radcliffe Institute, 1970. Mimeographed.

Tobias, Sheila, ed. *Female Studies I: A Collection of College Syllabi and Reading Lists.* Pittsburgh, Pa.: KNOW, INC., September 1970.

DUE